Journey Through The Dark Woods

Wayne Borns

FOREWORD BY
Alex Comfort

The Howe Street Press
Seattle, Washington

Library of Congress Cataloging in Publication Data

Burns, Wayne, 1918–
  Journey through the dark woods.

  Includes index.
  1. Burns, Wayne, 1918–
  2. College teachers––
United States––Biography. I. Title.
PR55.B8A34 1982   378'.12'0924 [B]
ISBN 0-9609666-0-9   82-15822

ISBN 0-9609666-0-9
Library of Congress No.: 82-15822

Copyright 1982 © by Wayne Burns

Published by The Howe Street Press
        212 East Howe Street
        Seattle, Washington 98102

Printed in the United States of America

Acknowledgments.

M<small>UCH</small> of my indebtedness is to those whose names appear in the following pages. George Bluestone, one of my oldest and closest friends, does not appear by name because I intended, right up to the very last minute, to include his "Wayne Burns as Teacher" (*Paunch*, #46–47) in an appendix to the present book. I am indeed sorry that practical considerations have prevented me from including this essay, since it is, apart from my place in it, a remarkably perceptive discussion of the art of teaching.

Irving Howe, Donna Gerstenberger, and Roger Sale read the first half of the book in manuscript, and their criticism helped me to clarify the ultimate objectives of my journey. I am also much indebted to those friends and former students who gave me their advice and support throughout the writing of the book—Monte Bolstad, Gerald Butler, John Doheny, James Flynn, Ian Gordon, Hugh Remash, and Jerald Zaslove. Although Michael Steig, Everett Greiman, and William Myers did not see the manuscript until it was essentially complete I have been much encouraged by their enthusiastic responses—especially William Myers' insistence, whether justified or not, that I "shouldn't change a word."

To Robert B. Heilman I owe a special debt of gratitude. Despite his profound disagreements with my approach to literature and teaching, he still managed to express his criticism of the manuscript with so much sympathy and insight that, if space had permitted and he had been willing, I should have liked to include his entire commentary.

My indebtedness to Alex Comfort extends to every phase of my journey. He understood, from the very beginning, where I was trying to go in the book and he did everything he could to help me get there. More important still, he understood why, in those instances when I could not follow his advice, I had to write in my own way.

And if teaching consists of resituating the text from world to classroom, then classroom becomes a new or additional grounding of the work, a new place for the apprehension of meaning, a new social and cultural situation for the literary event. Here seems to me to lie the peculiarity — and the extraordinary richness — of the subject: to talk about literature is inevitably to talk about what literature itself talks about. To engage it as an event in culture, in society, in history, is to engage all that is implied by it, all that is compacted within it— not only the breadth and depth of its allusions, but its special pressures upon private existence. These are not natural facts we have to deal with, but cultural facts: not crystals for analysis but formed interpretations of being which lend themselves to, which demand, further interpretation — not only of themselves but of our own beings through them.

Alan Trachtenberg

We can look in the real novels, and there listen-in . . . to the low, calling cries of the characters, as they wander in the dark woods of their destiny.

D. H. Lawrence

to the students
who braved the dark woods with me

Foreword

In universities now dedicated (it appears) to the instruction of MBA's and termites, there are still teachers—teachers as opposed to instructors. An instructor coaches. He may incidentally illuminate the subject, but, if he does, it is a work of supererogation. A teacher, by contrast, while he instructs, uses his own idiosyncrasy to show his students that the subject has importances beyond the getting of grades. By making them look through his own spectacles, however distorting, he shows them that there is more than one view. I had good teachers at school. They ranged from an ex-cavalry major to a Rudolf Steinerite who made his own neckties: the teaching lay in the variety, as well as in the qualities they had as instructors.

Wayne Burns is a teacher, and this book is about the hardships of being such. Teachers are unpopular with doctrinaire pupils, because they raise doubts; unpopular with administrators because such have in their minds the image of the Nabisco bandconveyor turning out educated gingerbread-men. Good students, however, love them. They called Burns "The Baron," and ensured his reward by peopling both writing and English studies with Burns disciples.

You, the reader, may be passionately interested in *what* Burns tried to teach his pupils about English literature, and how his approach differed in substance from Leavis or Northrop Frye or Tom Dick and Harry. Or you may not give a damn for the sub-stance of the scholarly disputations in which he engaged and still find this Odyssey fascinating, because the perils of this Odysseus did not spring from what he was teaching but from how he went about teaching it. Whatever he had been teach-ing—except possibly physics or mathematics, where originals are privileged and the admin side can't understand what they are talking about—he would have excited the same conformist aggro: it is the person of the teacher which is upsetting, not the teaching. One could even define a teacher as someone who upsets people, and a Great Teacher (Socrates? T.H. Huxley?) as someone who upsets a lot of people, though the test is not sym-metrical—one does not become a great teacher simply by virtue of creating enemies. But it helps, and one also creates oneself friends, of whom, in Wayne Burns' case, I count myself one. I was never his pupil; though he and his pupils have written perceptively about stuff I have written, I scratch no backs, and I own a distrust for books about books and the writers of books about books. Burns would value, I think, my appreciation of him as a critic (he is a good and original one) and I almost hesitate to tell him that the Burns who appeals to me even more is Burns the academic buccaneer, by Gully Jimson out of Roxana, whom I detect below the professorial surface, barely confined by commonroom propriety—he would be the kind of Don on which Cambridge has grown great. One may not care a hoot for Rageneau's verse and still root for Cyrano when he takes on all comers: one may not care what D.H. Lawrence had in mind, and still enjoy Burns' gigantomachia with bone-heads, student radicals, the Ossified University, American unscholar-ship and *hoc genus omne nugarum. Floreat.*

Contents

Introduction

MANY years ago, in the late thirties and early forties, there was a rebellious yet naive and idealistic young man—a kind of a cross between Hardy's Jude and Celine's Ferdinand—who believed that universities were "heavenly cities," that, consequently, to become a professor in a university would be the greatest thing he could do. And for him it was. Although his experiences in numerous universities obliged him to modify his vision of heavenly cities he finally made his way to an English department in which his inability, or his refusal, to get into line academically was not an insuperable handicap—a department in which he could go his own way in everything from his teaching to his research and writing. In this department he flourished—especially as a teacher. And he continued to find his ultimate fulfillment in the classroom, which was for him not so much a place for imparting knowledge or techniques as a place where, in his really good classes, he could meet and exchange ideas and impressions with students who were willing to go all the way with him in exploring what D.H. Lawrence calls "the dark woods of our destiny"—even when going all the way meant subjecting themselves to demands quite different from those they encountered in other literature classes. For the professor was not only encouraging the students to connect up the fiction with their own experience, he was encouraging them to make these connections in ways that invariably called into question their most cherished beliefs and ideals. That was why he called his approach Panzaic, after Sancho Panza in *Don Quixote*.

There came a time, however, the time of the Campus Revolution, when the great majority of the students no longer wanted to explore the dark woods; when they were no longer willing, paraphrasing Conrad, to immerse themselves in the destructive element; when, in fact, they were no longer willing to subject their new faiths to any form of critical scrutiny. Confronted with these militant students the professor could no longer teach as he had been teaching. Either he had to give up or drastically modify his approach to the classroom or fight it out with the students as best he could. He chose to fight, and for the most part it was a losing battle. But as the times and the students changed in the seventies, he eventually managed, in his undergraduate if not his graduate classes, to gain renewed acceptance for his Panzaic approach to literature. And now, after taking early partial retirement, and continuing to teach at Washington and at San Diego State, he feels that he has finally won back his own classroom.

Such, in outline, is the story I have to tell. At times it may read like an academic fairy tale, or a wish-fulfillment, yet it is neither fantasy nor wish-fulfillment. At other times it may read like fiction or autobiography, yet it is neither a novel, nor, in any ordinary sense, an autobiography. Except for chapter I, in which I try to explain my beginnings, the book is an historical account of my development as a teacher—an account in which I try to show, first of all, what it was like to teach literature in the old days, when it was still possible for a young professor to follow his own bent, even when, as in my own case, that bent brought him into direct conflict with everyone from his colleagues to his students.

Those days, needless to say, are gone forever—and with them the possibilities that I and other dissident spirits took advantage of in developing ourselves as teachers. I could not happen now. The way graduate schools in literature are set up today I could never, as a student, make my way through to the Ph.D. I just barely did then. Or if, by some strange chance, I did manage to secure a degree, no university would hire me and encourage me to become the teacher I became. There are too many brilliant young Ph.D.'s panting to do just what is being demanded of them. At this point it may seem as if I am trying to justify myself and my teaching by harking back to the good old days and bemoaning the awful present—as if I am, in short, embarking on an elaborate ego-trip. But I really am not. The trip I am undertaking is of a different nature altogether. My ego will be there all right, along with my regrets. I believed passionately in my teaching; I still do. Yet I recognize that I myself am an academic throwback, a neolithic carry-over from an earlier time. And I am not invoking the past, and my part in it, in order to exhort others to do now as I did then. The paths that I followed through the academic maze have long since been closed off.

But if I myself belong to a past time my approach to the teaching of literature does not. It is as valid now as it was in the fifties and early sixties; and if teachers can find ways to practice it in their classrooms without getting themselves fired, the students, or at least the undergraduate students, will respond as enthusiastically now as they did then. The proof for me—and it has come as a pleasant surprise after my years of discouragement—is that I have never had more responsive classes than those I have taught the past three years here at Washington and at San Diego State University. And I have had equally encouraging reports from those who have developed their own variations of the Panzaic in their own classrooms in other universities in this country and in Canada.

What stands in the way of Panzaic teaching, then, is no longer the students. Nor is it, in any blanket sense, university faculties or administrators, many of whom would be quite willing, as individuals, to condone, or even go along with, any mode of teaching that is intellectually responsible—as the Panzaic most certainly is. But very few faculty members, very few administrators, can any longer think, much less function, as individuals. The pressures on them—the pressures that over the past fifteen years have forced them into denying or compromising their intellectual commitments—are so great that they can no longer think or act in any way that threatens the organizational structures (still called universities) which they inhabit. Indeed many of the younger professors have become so professionalized, so bureaucratized, and, for good reason, just so plain scared of losing their jobs, that they can no longer conceive of intellectual responsibility apart from or in contradiction to the institutional demands that have been imposed upon them from graduate school onwards.

Nevertheless it is my hope that a few unregenerate individuals in the universities will find my Panzaic approach stimulating; and it is my further hope that they may still find ways to incorporate some variation of the approach in their own teaching. *1984* is hard upon us. Yet so long as unregenerate teachers can still meet unregenerate students in isolated and as yet unbugged classrooms there is surely some hope for the future.

1

Discovering My Heavenly City

My TEACHING career began some forty years ago, in September, 1940, at Miami University, Oxford, Ohio. And since I intend this book to be more about my teaching than about me, in so far as the two can be separated, my original plan was to begin at this point, with my actual teaching, and either omit or just barely mention how I got there. A good enough plan, perhaps, if my getting there had been more straightforward. Then I could have mentioned my undergraduate work at Miami (1934–1938), my M.A. at Harvard (1939), my year of Ph.D. work at Duke (1939–1940), plus a few words about my special interests and accomplishments, and I would have been ready to discuss my teaching.

But my getting there, so far from being straightforward, may be described as so strange, so unorthodox, that, as one of my chairmen later remarked, it should never have been permitted to happen at all. By which he meant, of course, that I, as a teacher, should never have been permitted to happen at all. And if I had come along fifteen or twenty years later, when graduate schools were getting better organized, in all probability

I never would have been permitted to happen at all. But at the time I was permitted, on occasion even encouraged, to develop the strange tendencies that shaped my whole approach to teaching—tendencies that can hardly be understood without a few autobiographical notes.

I shall try to keep these notes brief and to the point, leaving out all or nearly all of the details that would be essential to a full autobiography, or an autobiographical novel. Such details, interesting as they are to me, and might be to a reader, would overwhelm the more analytic account of my emotional and intellectual development that I am trying to present here—not for its own sake, but for what it helps to explain about my teaching. I mention my steady girlfriend, for example, but I do not mention our early marriage; nor do I attempt to give any sense of the part she played in my life, from the time I was fourteen onwards. To do so would be to introduce complexities beyond the scope of my intentions here. And so it is with all of my close personal relationships, which I have only touched upon, and then for the most part analytically, as they contribute to those aspects of my development that I am trying to clarify.

My potential as a man, if Freud is right, had in large measure been determined by the time I was four or five. Yet there is little I can say about what I was like then that is not family hearsay or pure speculation. My father died when I was a year old and my mother and I went to live on a farm with my grandmother Juilleret, a strong woman, quite proud of her peasant and Huguenot origins, who took it upon herself to see that I was brought up according to her strict notions of right and wrong. If I misbehaved my grandmother would go put on her bogeyman clothes, including a black hat, a long black cloak, and some kind of black mask; then she would confront me and demand that I correct my ways. I think perhaps there was also the implied threat that she would carry me off if I failed to obey. Yet I am not sure about this latter threat, primarily because just the sight of her was enough to frighten me into instant submission—until, on one occasion, she became so worried about the scare she was giving me that she let her voice take on a note of affectionate concern. At that moment it struck me that the bogeyman must be a lot like my grandmother, and therefore not so terrifying after all, and soon—as soon as my four-year-old mind could work things out—I began to realize that the bogeyman actually was my grandmother, and therefore not terrifying at all.

Many of the people whom I have told about my grandmother and the bogeyman have turned pale, or at the very least looked terribly sympathetic, as if they had at long last discovered where I began to go wrong. As I understand my experiences with the bogeyman, however, I am inclined to think their effects may have been salutary, since they not only taught me that bogeymen are not real and therefore not to be feared but also that creatures like bogeymen, such as Santa Claus, are merely good bogeymen, and not real either.

Quite possibly my unmasking of the bogeyman had no such effects, although I honestly believe that it did, but the fact remains that I went on, at what was, in the circumstances, an incredibly early age, to disbelieve in all the good and bad bogeymen that came my way—right up to the devil and God himself.

My childish disbelief, I must admit, could hardly have found expression if my Uncle Julius had not come to run my grandmother's farm when I was four. Although no one in my family had any formal schooling beyond, say, the eighth grade, my Uncle Julius, who had read quite a bit in the popular science and socialist pamphlets of the time, was by way of being a self-educated man; and it was he who first taught me to read, and then proceeded to give me lessons, almost every evening, on everything from politics to the world of nature and the stars and the universe. The lessons, I have since been told, were for the most part impassioned arguments against God and capitalism that for me, as a small boy, could have had little if any meaning. Yet I must have gained some sense of what he was saying, for I can still remember the time a few years later when my mother, in one of her rare attempts to get me started on the right path, took me to Sunday school—only to have me tell my Sunday school teacher that there was no God, that my Uncle Julius had said there wasn't, and he knew more than she did.

Following my mother's remarriage, when I was six, and our removal to the nearby village of Winchester, Ohio, I saw less and less of my Uncle Julius. But it was not my new stepfather who took his place as my heroic father-figure: it was my Uncle Mike, a worker in the Ford plant at Hamilton, Ohio. During the long summer vacations I spent with him and my Aunt Lizzie, from the time I was seven or eight till I was twelve or thirteen, he, too, plied me with socialist arguments. But what really won me over was not so much his arguments as his accounts of what he himself had been through—first, as a youth, before he left the Church, then as a bare-knuckles fighter in the back rooms of local saloons, then as a working man trying to fight the union breakers and the National Guard. When he took me swimming and we undressed in the bathhouse I could actually see the old wounds—where he had been chopped in the side by a man wielding an axe in a dark basement, where he had been stabbed in the ass by a bayonet while he was on strike. And when I got to go with him to Barney O'Raden's place even the gangsters like big Ed Zwick remembered what a great fighter Mike O'Brien had been. So when he told me that "they" were always out to get you, that the only way you could survive was by being tougher and smarter than they were, it went awfully deep—far deeper really than his socialist arguments.

For I already had a fairly well-developed notion of who "they" were. Even in grade school, thanks to my Uncle Julius as well as my Uncle Mike, I had begun to sense that the Sunday school maxims we were being taught at home and at school were a lie; that the people who spouted these maxims the most piously were often the greatest hypocrites; that the preacher's daughter, for instance, who called me a filthy boy when I used four-letter words in public was quite willing to go behind the barn with me when no one was looking; that my best friend's mother, for all her seeming strictness, was playing around with the guy who lived next door; that our scoutmaster, who made such a show of his moral rectitude, managed to ride our back-sides every time he played basketball with us.

Then, as I grew older, my sense of the discrepancies between what people and things were supposed to be like and what they were actually like became ever more acute, until I was well on the way to becoming a sort of hillbilly version of Stephen Dedalus, but with no religious teachings that I could believe in or revolt from, and with no sense that there were any intellectual or moral alternatives that weren't either simple-minded or phony.

Luckily for me there were things I passionately liked to do (primarily baseball, basketball, hunting, fishing) yet if I found these sports soul-satisfying they still did not in themselves provide me with a way out of the Sunday school pieties. On the contrary, it was just about impossible to engage in these sports without submitting to the pietistic attitudes that surrounded them. On one occasion, for example, when our high school basketball team was playing a team from Cincinnati that was, on paper, much better than we were, I made a statement in the local drugstore to the effect that our chances of winning were pretty slim, that we would be lucky if they didn't run up a big score on us. At this point the school principal asked me if I were willing to bet on the other team (a nickel against a dollar); and when I took him up on it, he promptly reported the incident to the coach, and I was not only benched for the game but charged with everything from moral turpitude (i.e., intending to throw the game) to Communist proclivities, the latter charge stemming, perhaps, from the run-ins I had been having with the principal in his social studies class.

Nor did my reaction to these charges help matters, since, to my boyish way of thinking, they were not just silly but vicious. Anyone who knew me, I felt, must know that I couldn't throw a game for any amount of money. And many people, including my teammates and the coach, did know, although they finally succumbed to the argument that my action was nevertheless foolish or reckless, that I somehow had to be taught a lesson, which was, of course, that everyone has to abide by the rules, no matter how silly or inadequate they may prove to be in a given situation.

Such rules, such lessons, were to me absurd, and I never could accept them. The best I could do was to accept the fact that, in most instances, I had to pretend to accept them. Perhaps, if I had been brought up differently, if I had been subjected to rules and lessons at home, I might have had less trouble accepting those that society imposed. But the only rules I had known were those imposed by my grandmother and the bogeyman when I was a mere child. After my grandmother my upbringing was that of an only child raised by a doting mother and almost equally doting aunts and uncles (and later supported by a loving stepsister, a selfless girlfriend, and a permissive stepfather) who gave me free rein in just about everything. More than that, they stood behind me in all my encounters with the outside world, in the process letting me know that they were always on my side, always there to love and support me, no matter what. When, for example, I had a serious run-in with the scoutmaster at the age of fourteen and was kicked out of the Boy Scouts, for what was labelled "violent insubordination" my mother not only supported me, she talked my stepfather into moving to another town (Georgetown, Ohio) so that I wouldn't have to bear the brunt of the censure that the good citizens of the town, young and old alike, were visiting upon me.

By almost any accepted standard, I was, in the words of the local townspeople, "spoiled rotten." Indeed some of them went so far as to predict that I would "end up in the state pen"—a prediction, incidentally, that I came perilously close to fulfilling later on when I became a non-religious conscientious objector in World War II. At the time, though, such predictions and comments didn't faze me: their effect was rather to make me even more defiant.

By the time I was fourteen, or perhaps fifteen, I was also finding new and wonderful justifications for my rebellious defiance in the novels I had begun reading when, by chance, I inherited a complete library from a distant uncle. Although I had already done quite a bit of reading, at least for a boy with my background, I had never, in fiction, got beyond the novels in the school library such as *Robinson Crusoe, Silas Marner,* and *When Knighthood Was in Flower.* And while I found these novels mildly interesting they hardly prepared me for what I found in my new library, which included more or less complete sets of Victor Hugo, Zola, and Balzac (all in English) along with odd volumes of English and American fiction ranging from *The Term of His Natural Life* to *Winesburg, Ohio.* The effect of these novels (and through my years in high school I read more of them than now seems possible) was so tremendous, in so many different ways, that I hardly know how to suggest how much they meant to me.

In certain instances, as might be expected, their first and most powerful effect derived from their treatment of sex—which in many of the novels, from Zola to Sherwood Anderson, went so much further than anything I had ever seen in print. In part, at least, my interest was undeniably prurient: even now I can recall scenes from *Madame Bovary,* for example, that were, as I then read them, pornographic. But for the most part my responses, even to what was directly sexual, were more complex than that. I was, for one thing, amazed and pleased to discover that I need no longer think of myself as sexually depraved—an impression that I had originally got from my grandmother (when she reprimanded me for sneaking underneath the girls' dresses, when I was four, to kiss them on their thighs), and that some of the townspeople I have spoken of had done their best to confirm. Not that I was terribly worried. It was just that I felt less confident in defying the sexual rules than I had in my other acts of defiance. And I was defying the rules, lax as they were in the hillbilly towns I grew up in, rather flagrantly, by getting myself involved in sexual situations that the townspeople simply could not accept. In all these situations, as in my encounters with the scoutmaster and the school principal, I was once again being taught lessons, and once again I was refusing to learn.

Nevertheless I remained a bit shaky in my refusal until—thanks to what the novels showed me about people's motives—I came to realize that nearly all the things I suspected, but had tried to keep from believing, were actually true: that the preacher who took it upon himself to warn my girlfriend about my sexual proclivities had sexual proclivities of his own; that the sheriff's deputy who accused me (a mere boy) of consorting with prostitutes was endeavoring to cover up the sexual brutalities he had practiced on the very same prostitutes. And so it was with all my experiences and observations: the effect of the novels was to verify my deepest suspicions about what "they" (the scoutmaster, the preacher, the school principal, the deputy sheriff) were trying to do to me and everyone else who either could not or would not accept their rules and maxims. For the novels (from *The Term of His Natural Life* to *The Toilers of the Sea* to *Winesburg* to *Main Street*) clearly showed who "they" were, what "they" were up to, and how "they" were up to it. More important still, the novels showed that the people they were trying to subdue were heroes and heroines who had right, if not might, on their side. And while I did not see myself as equal to these superior beings, I could nevertheless see that my struggles closely resembled theirs—so closely, in fact, that if they were right in their struggles, then I was right in mine.

It might seem, therefore, that the novels, at least as I read them, merely bore out what I myself believed, and what my loved ones had for so long been telling me: that I was always right. But there was a difference: the heroes of fiction weren't right just because they themselves believed they were, or because their loved ones thought so too. Even as a child I had come to recognize that my mother was partial, that when she or my Aunt Lizzie or my Uncle Mike declared me right, no matter what scrape I got myself into, they were speaking out of love (mixed, in my Uncle's case, with hatred of the capitalist system). And I wanted something more: I wanted what might be called reason; that is, I wanted to know, not just to feel; I wanted, for example, to know that I was right when I defied the scoutmaster, the townspeople wrong when they defended him.

And the novels gave me reason, or, more precisely, I derived reason from them. Through my identification with the heroes and my consequent sense of their dilemmas and difficulties, as they made their way through worlds similar to my own, I somehow fashioned a workable sense of right and wrong. Not always a fully adequate sense, I must hasten to acknowledge, since I at times managed to justify thoughts and actions that were of a piece with those I found objectionable—as, for instance, the time I bloodied the nose of one of the local homosexuals for making a harmless pass at me. Yet if I somehow managed to justify myself in this instance, I still felt uneasy. I know I did because of the way such instances continued to worry me. And I think they worried me because I could never quite square my thoughts and actions with those of the heroes in the novels. Would Dickens' Pip have done what I did? Or Eugene Aram? Or the heroes (whose names I can no longer recall) of *The Toilers of the Sea* or *The Term of His Natural Life*?

I mention these heroes because these novels were among my favorites. But my choices do not matter too much because I am not trying to suggest that I was strongly influenced by specific novels, or that I could distinguish the huge qualitative differences between *Great Expectations* and *Eugene Aram*. The effects of my novel reading seem to have been cumulative. I could go from *Toilers of the Sea* to *Madame Bovary* to Kipling's short stories to *Sons and Lovers* without realizing how far apart, in time as well as depth, these various works actually were. In part I could do this, I suppose, because I had no sense of literary history, or, for that matter, literary distinctions of any kind. So long as a novel created a world filled with people and conflicts and situations that I could somehow relate to my own—and just about every novel in the collection I inherited did that, I feel sure—it was providing me with the revelations as well as the reason that I needed to understand and justify myself in my struggles with my own world. For me, indeed, the novels took the place of the moral and religious precepts that the boys and girls I knew were getting at home and in school.

During these boyhood years I also saw a tremendous number of movies—my parents ran movie houses in the various small towns we lived in—and I derived considerable enjoyment from some of them. But few, if any, affected me in anything like the way the novels did. After I had sat through two or more showings of even the better movies of the day (as I often had to do in connection with my work in the movie houses) their simplistic formulas invariably began to show through—the goody-goody good guys and the good-hearted bad guys all mixed up over the good girl or the good bad girl; or, alternatively, any or all of the above mixed up in a social theme that invariably ended up in Sunday school moralizing. This is not to deny that I found many of the scenes in the movies powerful or compelling: Hollywood could always present violence and shooting and death awfully well. Nor is it to deny that there may have been a few really good movies that I missed or have forgotten. My point is only that, despite my intense and extended exposure to the movies, they gave me nothing comparable to what I was getting from the novels.

Had I not gone to college my reliance on fiction might have continued on indefinitely. But college was, for me, a great and marvelous awakening. In my courses and my reading (especially in history, and philosophy and sociology) I was amazed to discover that the great thinkers of the past and present had already thought all the rebellious thoughts I had been trying to think; that they had all kinds of evidence, all kinds of arguments, which provided all kinds of answers to the questions I had for so long been agonizing over. More amazing still, there were professors so different from the teachers I had encountered in high school that I could hardly believe it; professors who were, for all their learning, willing and even anxious to discuss my questions in terms that I could understand.

At this point, in an effort to express more fully what my undergraduate years at Miami meant to me, I am tempted to suggest that I actually found in Miami the University that Jude first envisaged in *Jude the Obscure*. But this comparison, though it may in some respects be apt, finally tends to be misleading. For the truth is, I did not approach Miami with any great expectations. Mainly I was just curious: I wanted to see what college was like, and since no one from Georgetown ever went to college unless he was going to become a lawyer or a doctor, I signed up for pre-law (majoring in English) without having the slightest notion of what I was getting myself into. But once my classes started, where they were leading in a practical sense no longer mattered: all that mattered was the classes themselves, for they opened up a new world to me in much the same way that my earlier reading of novels had opened up new worlds, the main difference being that the world the classes opened up was one I could actually live in. To me at the time it really did seem as if I had discovered my heavenly city, and I wanted to stay there always. To be there and just read and study and talk and figure things out.

In other words I wanted to become a professor, though of what, I had no clear idea. While I was graduating as an English major (having dropped the pre-law category early on) I had to acknowledge that, with a few notable exceptions, my English courses had proved much less exciting than those I had taken in such subjects as evolution, abnormal psychology, and yes, even English constitutional law. But I was committed to English if I wanted to continue on to graduate school in the following year; and in any case I had come to believe (thanks to A. W. Craver, one of the English professors at Miami for whom I had the deepest admiration) that English offered the professor more freedom of interpretation than any other academic subject; that, in English, the professor could go places no other professor could go.

It was with notions such as these that I set off for Harvard graduate school, hoping to find there the best and hardest and greatest of all the heavenly cities. And I was not altogether disappointed: from all I was able to tell at the time (and later when I taught there) Harvard may well be the ultimate heavenly city. But the English department was something else. The big names were there all right, one, for instance, giving a seminar in James Fenimore Cooper (as if Cooper were a serious novelist) and then not even bothering to read all of Cooper's novels. Indeed, of the courses I took, the only one that I would characterize as really outstanding was E. J. Simmons' year-long course in the English novel, in which I learned a great deal not only about English fiction but also—and this was even more important to me at the time—about Marxist criticism.

My very first literature course at Miami had left me vaguely dissatisfied with what the professor was calling criticism, and I had become increasingly dissatisfied in the years following, since neither my courses nor my own reading seemed to provide me with a means of resolving my primary critical questions, of which the most basic, perhaps, were those that turned on the conflict between form and content. Of course I had acquainted myself with the more obvious modes of resolving the con- flict—modes that I discussed at length with my fellow stu- dents and professors. But to no real avail: either they tried to resolve matters on what seemed to me to be inadequate or hope- lessly tenuous grounds, or, most disconcerting of all, they tried to argue that the conflict was only a seeming one, that once I arrived at the proper aesthetic position the conflict would simply disappear. While I could see the logic of this latter argument, I could also see—and this is what made it so dis- concerting—that the literature which meant the most to me would have to disappear too; either that or it would, at the very least, have to be relegated to some inferior position, along with the literature of social protest that was popular in the thirties.

Then—thanks to E.J. Simmons, and later the bookstores on Harvard Square—I began finding in Marxist criticism the kind of aesthetic that I had been looking for—an aesthetic that would enable me to insist first upon the human significance of a work (*i.e.*, its content) without committing myself to a particular ideological position that would render matters of form secon- dary or even irrelevant. Or, put less abstractly, what I wanted was a way of looking at literature that would enable me to hang on to the works of the novelists and playwrights (from Zola and Shaw to James Farrell and John Steinbeck and Clifford Odets) that I was finding most meaningful without apologizing for their "form" or having to defend their work on ideological grounds. For I could see, even then, that literature tied to ideology could never be more than highly sophisticated propaganda.

To anyone unacquainted with Marxist criticism it may

seem strange, perhaps even contradictory, that I should have found in it, the ultimate ideological criticism, the means of avoiding the pitfalls of such criticism. But there is a simple answer to this seeming contradiction. Marxist critics and aestheticians, from Plekhanov onwards, had been constantly up against the difficulty of squaring their sense of aesthetic quality with their political beliefs and commitments, and in their efforts to resolve this difficulty they had developed an aesthetic that stretches its ideological roots so far that they hardly seem ideological at all. Later on I would come to see Marxist criticism differently. Primarily I would come to see that, for all its dialectical subtleties, it had not really severed the direct ideological connection, only disguised its workings; that even Trotsky, in his undeniably great criticism of Celine's *Journey to the End of the Night*, finally had to stop short when the revolutionary implications of the novel posed a direct threat to his own ideology. But, to repeat, such reservations as these came much later. When I first encountered Marxist criticism at Harvard, and for several years afterward, I believed that I had found, if not *the* answers, at least the way to work out the answers to all my critical difficulties.

And so, when I went to Duke University in the following year, after deciding that I just could not accept Harvard's philological requirements for the Ph.D., I went as a graduate student version of a Marxist critic, never realizing, in my academic naivete, that the Marxist criticism which had been commonplace at Harvard would not be acceptable, or even understood, at Duke. Indeed many of my fellow students and at least some members of the faculty immediately presumed that I was a party member, disguised as a graduate student, who was more interested in recruiting for the party than in graduate work. Needless to say they were totally mistaken. While I undoubtedly had some beliefs and proclivities that might be labelled Communist, including those I had carried over from my boyhood sessions with my Uncle Julius and my Uncle Mike, I had not, at that time, gone much further to the left politically than the liberals I had met and talked with at Harvard.

The misunderstandings occasioned by my being mistaken

for a party member might therefore have passed without serious consequences if a real party member had not appeared on the scene. This man, a brilliant philosopher and theologian from Canada who was somehow connected with the school of divinity at Duke, took the trouble to look me up and sympathize with me on my plight in the English department. Then, after deciding that I might be a valuable recruit, he set about introducing me (along with a few others he had chosen from various graduate schools at Duke and the University of North Carolina) to the fundamentals of Communist doctrine and practice. Intellectually I had something of a head start, through the reading I had done in Marxist criticism; and while I soon began to have serious doubts about ever being able to become a cog in the Communist machinery, which clearly was what becoming a party member meant, I still felt drawn, quite powerfully, by the thought that I would be joining with others like myself all over the world—other men and women who were uniting to overcome the people and forces that I had, till then, been struggling against alone.

It was a hopelessly romantic view, going back to my boyhood struggles in Georgetown, and to the notions of socialism I had picked up from my Uncle Julius and my Uncle Mike. And my grownup efforts to translate my boyish feelings of personal rebellion into an enthusiastic acceptance of the Communist cause must have appeared quite ineffectual to my Communist mentor. In any event he soon became so unhappy with what he called my incorrigible lack of intellectual discipline, which he defined as my penchant for raising questions when no questions were called for, that he told me, politely but firmly, that I would never make a Communist; that I was, in fact, so much of a bourgeois individualist that I could never become anything but an anarchist.

Quite a bit later I came to realize the truth of this last observation. At the time, however, I was merely chastened, not entirely convinced—although, on a practical level, I had no choice but to accept my unfitness for party membership and to devote my full energies to my graduate work. But that, too, went badly, almost from the start, primarily because I insisted on bringing Marxist critical theories and techniques into seminar discussions and term papers. My situation in the department consequently went from bad to worse until, towards the end of the spring semester, Paull Baum, who was then chairman, called me in to straighten out matters. He began by telling me that I would be coming up for my Ph.D. exams fall semester; that I should therefore know that in all likelihood I would fail the exams, not because I lacked ability but because I lacked discipline. And when I pointed out that "discipline," the way he seemed to be using the word, might be equated with docility, he agreed, then went on to concede that even he could not pass the exams if his examining professors were unfavorably disposed towards him. My only hope, he explained, lay in convincing my professors and the department that I recognized the error of my ways, and would now accept their guidance in the spirit in which they were offering it. I had, he conceded further, done excellent work for Don Cameron Allen (in whose seminar I had, for my term project, edited *The Three Ladies of London*) and if I were to continue on in the same vein in my own field, by expressing my desire to edit some Rossetti manuscripts for my Ph.D. thesis, he would be happy to let everyone know about my change of mind and heart. "Otherwise," he said, "you would do well to return to Harvard, or, better still, go to Iowa, where they even give Ph.D.'s for creative writing."

For Professor Baum's candor I was, and remain, sincerely grateful. He could very easily have just let me fail; instead he put everything right on the line—from the way the department saw me to what its demands would be. But the demands themselves, as Professor Baum represented them, were another matter, since he was, I believed, demanding nothing less than the sacrifice of my moral and intellectual integrity. In other words he was demanding, in academic terms, what my Communist mentor had demanded in political terms, what my scoutmaster and my high school principal had demanded years before in social terms. The big difference was that I had never really believed in the Scouts or in high school (and in any case my reactions had been those of a boy); nor had I really believed in Communism, much as I had tried. But I had come to believe in the freedom of thought I found at Miami and Harvard—so much so, as I have tried to suggest, that they took on the aura of heavenly cities—and I entered Duke with the firm belief that it would be free and heavenly too. And while the difficulties I encountered in the English department, almost from the beginning, had been somewhat disillusioning, they had not prepared me for Professor Baum's demands, which, as I understood them, rendered graduate work at Duke, or any place like Duke, farcical.

My disillusionment at the time was so complete that I could not bring myself to consider the possibility of going to some other graduate school. What I wanted, or thought I wanted, was to get away completely, to erase any lingering hopes I might have for an academic career. Yet none of the positive alternatives that were open to me seemed worthy of serious consideration. I could perhaps have done very well financially as a tennis pro (I had one quite good offer from a Cincinnati tennis club); or I could have gone into the sporting goods business (with Cincinnati Sporting Goods). But such jobs seemed meaningless, or nearly so, and simply making money seemed to be a terrible waste of time and effort—much as I liked some of the things money could provide. So what I finally did, after leaving Duke, was take over management of a movie theatre my family was opening in Russell, Kentucky, not because the job was challenging or rewarding, but because it gave me time to read and think about the books I had been obliged to pass over or skim through in graduate school.

For a time during that summer of 1940 I thoroughly enjoyed my solitary reading and thinking. After completing *Don Quixote*, for example, or *War and Peace*, books that I had never had time to read before, I felt terribly mature, and more than a little self-satisfied, as I tended, somewhat romantically I'm afraid, to see myself as a latter-day hero suffering nobly and alone for his intellectual integrity. Yet as the summer wore on my isolation became less and less romantic, more and more real, and by September, the month in which I had always returned to school, I was beginning to reconsider the possibility of some kind of return to some kind of university. Not as a graduate student—I was by no means ready for that—but as some kind of teacher.

Then my next thought was to try Miami, the one place I wanted to go most, on the off chance that they might have a last-minute opening. And because time was so short, and I was so anxious, I just went, without calling or writing—to find the English department so desperately in need of an instructor that they hired me on the spot.

2

My Idyllic Apprenticeship and Its Not So Idyllic Accompaniments

My RETURN to Miami was, for me, a happy and even a triumphant homecoming. It didn't matter that my instructorship was only temporary and part-time and woefully ill-paid. I was so glad to be there, and to be accepted as a colleague by A. W. Craver and the other members of the English Department, that I would have accepted almost any terms.

Nor did it matter that my teaching schedule, once I had agreed to accept an extra section of English 100, was little short of brutal: five sections of Freshman Composition, with some thirty students in each section and with each of these students turning in a theme of three hundred words or more every week. Just getting through these papers was a full-time job in itself. I found myself reading themes at the dinner table, on the way to class, and, on one occasion, at a basketball game. Finally, though, the themes weren't as difficult as the inevitable repetitiousness in the class hours themselves, since, with five more or less identical sections, I often had to give the same lecture, or cover the same material, five different times in a single day.

And to make matters worse I did not, in the beginning, have

any great desire to teach. What I found so exciting about my return to Miami was not the prospect of becoming a teacher but rather the prospect of becoming a full-fledged member of an intellectual community—the only kind of intellectual community I had ever experienced. If I had been able to secure a life-time fellowship involving no teaching assignments (such as those offered by Oxford and Cambridge in the nineteenth century) that would have been ideal. Or if I had been acquainted with, and could have been accepted by, some other kind of intellectual community—say, for instance, the *Partisan Review* intellectuals in New York—I might have preferred them and writing to Miami or any other university and teaching. But such alternatives were beyond my ken. Miami was my heavenly city, and if I had to teach to stay there, I would.

Yet if I was determined I was also apprehensive. For I could see clearly enough, once I actually began meeting classes, that the ideas and attitudes which had got me into difficulties as a student might get me into even more serious difficulties as a teacher. To begin with, my attitude towards power. In the classroom the professor is always in a position of power, in some respects a position of nearly absolute power, and many professors (who may or may not be authoritarian personalities in the outside world) function as authoritarians in the classroom. They use their power to drill or whip their students into intellectual shape; and if they wield their whips skillfully enough, and have any sort of flair for their work, they often generate a full and positive response in their students.

For my own part, however, I could never, as a student, respond positively to such demands or to such professors—perhaps because both the demands and the professors called up memories of my boyhood encounters with my scoutmaster and my high-school principal. Nor could I, once I myself began teaching, assume an authoritarian role in the classroom, even when I could see that by doing so I might win over some recalcitrant students and accomplish some otherwise very desirable ends. At times, indeed, I had students come right out and demand, or beg for, more discipline, more whipping, more cajoling, or at the very least more fussing and carping, so that they could do better work. Yet I could never meet their spoken or unspoken demands. I was, in fact, incapable of meeting them, and therefore incapable of establishing the sense of connection between professor and student that accompanies such demands.

Perhaps, if I had been able to have faith in some political ideology, or philosophy, or religion, or morality, I might have been able to overcome my primary aversion to the exercise of power or discipline. Perhaps I could then have convinced myself that the ends might justify the means. But my attempt to join the Communist Party was the closest I could come to embracing a faith, and that attempt, as my Communist mentor pointed out, only served to show that I was constitutionally incapable of accepting any faith. And while my pacifist beliefs, for which I was to suffer through my second and third years at Miami, might at first blush seem to constitute an exception, the truth is that I did not hold these beliefs as a matter of faith. So far as I was concerned they were matters of intellectual conviction achieved through reasoning, and that is how I tried to present and defend them. I was not preaching, or even supporting, a cause or faith; I never tried to persuade anyone to become a pacifist, or to join or support a pacifist movement. I was, for better or worse, incapable of believing in a pacifist or any other movement.

Furthermore—and this may seem more disastrous for an English professor than any of my other disabilities—I could never even accept the seemingly innocuous belief that, in some measure, nearly all English professors cling to: the belief that literature is somehow morally and culturally ennobling; that at the very least such study will improve one's taste and thereby render him more sensitive and cultured and civilized. These words and the concepts for which they stood had given me no end of trouble as a student and I found them equally trouble-some when I began to teach. Good taste, for example, seemed to me little more than a sophisticated form of mass-mindedness, and my reservations about sensitivity and culture were much like E. M. Forster's reservations about democracy. I too could give only two cheers, and I had to accompany these cheers with so many doubts and qualifications that my cheers may have seemed more like jeers.

But this is not to say I was cynical. If I had been I might have been able to see the classroom as a theatre, the podium as a stage—the way so many English professors do. And I might then have tried to give witty and urbane lectures; or, alternatively, I might have tried to assume the role of a folksy cynic. The variations on the stagey roles are limitless, given enough cynicism and enough talent. But whatever their possibilities they were not for me, since I hadn't a smidge of either talent or cynicism. And it wasn't just that I lacked talent and somehow wished that I had it or could develop it: I not only didn't have it, I didn't want it. I didn't want to be witty and urbane and give polished lectures—even if that was what students wanted and appreciated and responded to.

It may seem at this point as if I have eliminated just about every motivation for becoming a teacher except that of imparting technical knowledge or skills. Yet the sad truth is that I had no burning desire to impart such knowledge or skills. Much of Freshman Comp (with its emphasis on rhetoric and grammar) necessarily involves this kind of teaching, and in my classes that first year at Miami I did what was required, though not with any great sense of accomplishment or satisfaction. Nor was I much more interested in this kind of teaching as it applied to the literature that we read: imparting the knowledge and skills that underlie literary criticism was, I could see, a necessary preliminary to any form of serious literary discussion, and I therefore felt obliged to do what I could by way of teaching such knowledge and skills in the classroom—once again, however, without any great sense of accomplishment or satisfaction.

ii

It was therefore without any of what are generally considered the essential motives and qualifications that I embarked on my teaching career. About the only positive thing I had going for me as a beginning teacher, apart from my routine academic qualifications, was my intellectual adventurousness—my sense that the classroom could and should be a place of intellectual excitement and adventure. It was not a matter of my wanting to do anything flamboyant or sensational. I had no inclination to use shock techniques on students—the way, for example, one of my colleagues did a few years later (when four-letter words were still shocking) by writing the word "fuck" on the blackboard. What I wanted, rather, was to proceed quietly and seriously, without dirty words, or jokes, or innuendos, to a full consideration of any and all serious issues that might arise in the classroom, no matter how outrageous or heretical the implications of such issues might prove to be.

In other words I wanted to do what the professors I had studied under (including even those I most admired) had not for one reason or another chosen to do. In some instances their evasiveness could, I believed, be attributed to their timidity or their conventionality or even their stupidity (professors are not always very bright); in other instances, however, their evasiveness had, I felt sure, been attributable to their sincere conviction that the classroom was simply not the place to discuss questions which might impinge seriously upon the faiths or beliefs of their students. I knew or surmised that this was their sincere conviction because, in many instances, they were quite willing, after class, to discuss the very questions and to consider the very implications that they had just evaded in class.

Later on I would discover, through my own experiences and observations, that there were still other reasons for what I considered evasiveness—reasons which had more to do with what the professors were trying to accomplish than with what they were trying to evade. At the time, however, I had little if any sense of these reasons, little if any sense of the difficulties that I myself, as a beginning teacher, would have to overcome in the classroom. While I could, as a practical matter, see that much of what I had to do in Freshman English, especially in grammar and rhetoric, might very well prove tedious, if not downright dull, I had really high hopes for what I might be able to do with the reading material in the course, since the prescribed text (*Patterns for Living*, edited by Campbell, Van Gundy, and Shrodes) seemed to offer possibilities for all manner of intellectual excitement. There were essays and poems plus a couple of plays, and, most important of all, fictional selections that might, I fondly believed, mean as much to the students as my boyhood reading had meant to me.

With stories as inherently provocative as Mark Schorer's "Boy in the Summer Sun," or Willa Cather's "Paul's Case," I felt confident that I could, just by telling the students that they were free to express their own reactions, get a meaningful discussion going. Yet my expectations were seldom if ever realized. The students themselves seemed intelligent enough, and willing, even anxious, to avail themselves of the chance to express their full reactions. But they didn't know how. And at that point I didn't know how to help them. Usually the best they could do, once they had settled on some character or moral issue, was a kind of round robin discussion in which they took turns setting forth the most banal generalities in the firm belief that they were expressing individual and highly personal responses. After even the tritest of their round robins they would leave the classroom feeling that they had participated in a meaningful discussion when, in point of fact, they had merely engaged in a classroom version of a bull session, or what in the sixties came to be called a rap session, in which they had trotted out their various prejudices or platitudes without so much as touching upon the serious issues that lay beneath the surface.

What they were doing, I can now see, was what they had been doing all their lives—in discussion groups, in bull sessions, and in classrooms. Which is, of course, what students and people generally are still doing. Technical matters apart we more and more live by cliches. At all levels and with only rare exceptions this is true. Many of us, for example, can no longer be said to have lives; we have cliched categories for our lives that we identify, with varying degrees of sophistication, as life styles. Just recently, in a class discussion of Tolstoy's "The

Death of Ivan Ilych," one of my undergraduates observed that Ivan Ilych's difficulties lay in his life style, that if Tolstoy had recognized this he could have given his story a happy ending. Whereupon another student, relieved to find that Tolstoy's novella might be comprehensible after all, since it turned on something familiar, something he understood, went on to suggest that Ivan Ilych would never have been injured at all if he had chosen a simple life style. And if I had permitted the discussion to continue along these lines we might well have had a rousing debate in which we would have turned "The Death of Ivan Ilych" into a problem for Dear Abby.

While such devastating oversimplications still give me a bit of a shock, they no longer overwhelm me the way they did when I first began teaching. For I have come to realize that students think and talk in cliches, not because they are stupid, or perverse, or lazy, but because they don't have anything else to think and speak with. Consequently they will, when confronted with a work of serious fictional literature that cuts through or even attacks their cliches (as all serious literature inevitably does) be at a loss to understand what the work is saying. It won't make any sense to them until they can somehow reduce its complexity to one or another of their cliched conceptions, the way my two students reduced "The Death of Ivan Ilych" to a question of "life styles." Students have to do this, I now realize, and the teacher has to let them. But—and this is the crucial point—he can never let them stop there: he must somehow get the students to see and acknowledge the discrepancies between their cliches and the complexities of the literature, between their "life style" and the life and death that Tolstoy presents in his novella. For the students can never gain a sense of life and death—even from Tolstoy—so long as they see life as a matter of style.

As a beginning teacher, however, I had no way of knowing that the students had to have their cliches before they could work through them. I wanted to deny them their cliches out of hand and altogether, in the hope that they would then be free to respond directly to what the work of literature was trying to say. But freeing them in this way was like dumping them in the middle of the Atlantic and giving them the freedom to swim ashore. Unless I was going to lecture, and thus do the reading for them, or, alternatively, unless I was going to provide them with ready-made formulas (such as those soon to be provided by the New Critics) I had to find some way to help the students find a way to move from their world into the infinitely more complex worlds of Tolstoy and other serious writers.

And since the students could hardly make this move without abandoning, for the moment at least, the comfort and security they had found in their cliches for the shocks and uncertainties that serious writing inevitably produces, I also had to help them find a reason for moving as well as a way to move. For who would trade comfort for discomfort, security for insecurity, unless he believed that his discomfort and insecurity could yield some ultimate good. Then, as now, students were offered any number of stock answers in which ultimate good was equated with everything from "art appreciation" to culture with a capital "K" and no "e." But since I could never accept those equations for myself I could hardly expect the students to accept them. Later on in my teaching I would, with the help of D.H. Lawrence and other critics, work out some critical equations that would meet the students' needs. But in the beginning I couldn't do much more than offer them a Marxist version of the ultimate good (brought up to date with quotes from *The Partisan Review*) that they could hardly understand, much less accept.

iii

By my own standards, then, my initial efforts as a teacher of fiction were, to say the least, inadequate. I knew they were inadequate—even when the students seemed quite happy with what we were doing in class. For that matter, if there had been any student evaluations in those days I would undoubtedly have received a fairly high rating. Students always appreciate sincerity and effort in a teacher, and when they find that he also loves his subject they appreciate him even more. But for me it wasn't enough to be appreciated as an amiable enthusiast. I wanted to help the students see the fiction as I saw it, so that it might prove as exciting and meaningful to them as my early reading of novels had been for me.

Yet if I could not in my early classes even begin to realize this aim in teaching fiction I did come close to realizing my more modest aims in teaching the non-fictional selections in *Patterns for Living*. My success with these writings (which ranged all the way from Joseph Wood Krutch's "Love—or the Life and Death of a Value" to Harold Laski's "Why I am a Marxist" to Bertrand Russell's "Munich Rather than War") was almost instantaneous; primarily, I have since come to recognize, because nonfiction, being more abstract than fiction, and consisting mainly of ideas, does not pose the same kind of threat to the reader that fictional literature does. The ideas may be disturbing or even shocking, but still they are only ideas, and (the sciences apart) there are always other ideas, seemingly every bit as cogent, to counter the disturbing ones. And even if the countering ideas prove inadequate, even if the disturbing ideas cannot be denied, the worst that can happen is that one has to change one's mind—a difficult process, admittedly, but nothing like as difficult as that which fiction demands. A student reading Bertrand Russell's "Munich Rather than War," for example, may at first be shocked into trying to find counter arguments; then he can either relieve his shock by accepting these counter arguments, or, if they prove inadequate, he can change his mind. The same student reading "The Death of Ivan Ilych," on the other hand, has no such alternatives, for Tolstoy is not expressing *ideas* about life and death, he is portraying, in terrifying detail, the death of a man much like ourselves in a world much like our own; and if the student recognizes these likenesses, he must change not just his mind but his sense of himself and the world he lives in.

Once again these were distinctions that I did not recognize at the time. Yet if I did not, in my inexperience, understand why the students found the non-fictional writings less threatening, and why, on the positive side, they were more receptive, more willing to have their stereotypes challenged, I soon learned to recognize and take advantage of their willingness and receptivity—to lead them into intellectual territories that they had previously been reluctant to explore. And if some of the students balked at my efforts to bring out the full implications of the essays on "love" and "Marxism" and " Munich," many did not; in any case even those who balked seemed to share at least some of the intellectual excitement that the class discussions generated. Indeed my treatment of the non-fictional writings proved so effective that I was soon trying to extend it to other work in the course. The non-fiction book report, on which we spent considerable time during the spring semester, seemed to offer the best possibility, and during my second year (actually my fourth semester) I formulated some rather elaborate plans for teaching the non-fiction report—plans that I later published in *College English* (December, 1943) under the title, "Creative Thinking in the Non-Fiction Book Report."

Looking back now I have to smile a bit, not only at my title, but at the naively mechanical way in which I set forth my plan. Nevertheless I am quoting the article at length, since it is the only firsthand piece of evidence I have that shows how I was thinking, and trying to teach, during my years at Miami:

> The writing of the book report usually required in freshman English has become in many colleges a meaningless task to both students and instructors. The nonfiction book reports seem particularly difficult to handle. The present writer, after conducting the nonfiction reports in the traditional ways, has finally hit upon a method that gets results—three very important results. One of the primary functions of the nonfiction report should be to encourage the student to think objectively about all kinds of human problems—to do what James Harvey Robinson calls "creative thinking." A second important function, and a necessary corollary to the first, should be to enable the student to read with understanding. And, finally, since reading and thinking are of no great value unless the resultant ideas can be adequately communicated, the third function of the book report should be

to inculcate better writing habits. The present plan, though it emphasizes thinking, performs to a certain degree all three functions.

A few suggestions from John Dewey's *How We Think* are basic to the plan. Dewey believes that there are five distinct steps in reflective thought:

> (i) a felt difficulty; (ii) its location and definition; (iii) suggestion of possible solution; (iv) development by reasoning of the bearings of the suggestion; (v) further observation and experiment leading to its acceptance or rejection; that is, the conclusion of belief or disbelief.

These suggestions, together with Dewey's explanation of them, lay the groundwork for the "creative thinking" book report.

The plan itself is a simple one. Only four steps are necessary: (1) testing the student's thought reactions, (2) choosing a proposition and requesting the student to write an essay in support of his thought reactions, (3) selecting a book (or books) that fits the student's subject and his thought reactions, and (4) assigning the book report. First, the students should be tested to find what their thought reactions are to a number of controversial propositions. Mody C. Boatright's *Accuracy in Thinking* contains exactly the type of test needed. His "self-test" works this way: He lists twenty-one propositions—*e.g.*, "Atheism is the only religion that frees the mind from fear" and asks the student to evaluate honestly each proposition according to the following key: "1. So obviously absurd that no further consideration is merited. 2. Improbable. 3. Debatable. 4. Probable. 5. So obviously true that further consideration is unnecessary." Then, after the student has evaluated the propositions, Mr. Boatright asks him to indicate whether or not some of his reactions were emotional ("E" if in some degree emotional; "U" if unemotional). This last step is helpful but not absolutely necessary here. If retained, it can be varied—perhaps for the better—by suggesting that the student classify his thought reactions according to James Harvey Robinson's four kinds of thinking. Also, for the present purposes, it might be well to add considerably to the number of propositions in the test. It is important that the topics be numerous and varied enough to appeal to the interests of all types of students.

Obviously, tests of this type cannot be scored objectively, but a "1" or a "5," for example, in answer to such a proposition as this, "Every college student in America should be required to read Marx's *Das Kapital*," is a fairly definite indication that the student's emotions are interfering with his thought processes—even if the student has not seen fit to label his reaction "emotional." The student making such an answer, if private consultation reveals that he is definitely interested in the problems involved, should then be asked to write an essay in support of his opinion—an essay in which he clarifies and records his own ideas in preparation for the coming encounter with the professional opposition. But a proposition should not be assigned too hastily. The student must be led to choose a proposition in which he is definitely interested and about which he has decided opinions. Otherwise the instructor will later find himself at a loss to discover a book sufficiently challenging to jar the average student out of his unthinking complacency.

Now, assuming that the student has written a satisfactory essay in defense of his reaction to a given proposition, the instructor's problem is to suggest one or more books that disagree with the student's reaction. Just any book will not do. Careful selection is necessary—even though the instructor may have to do some library work in what may be strange fields.

Finally, after the student has studied the book or books assigned and has reconsidered his original stand, he is ready to write the book report. The nature and form of this report can, of course, vary considerably. In practice, the present writer has suggested that a student, to receive credit for a good report, should include the following material: (1) a brief restatement of his original stand as presented in the first essay, (2) a fair and accurate presentation of the pertinent arguments found in the book or books, (3) a comparison of his own arguments with those of the book or books, (4) a statement of his final conclusions on the problem, and (5) an estimate of the extent to which the reading has changed his mind.

Such, in brief, is the procedure. But whether it looks good on paper or not, the final proof of its validity lies in the results which have been obtained in practice. Three different instructors have tried the plan on seven different classes and have found that it brings forth not only surprising improvements in thinking but also recognizable improvements in reading and writing. The student reports themselves, were it possible to quote them, would best substantiate these claims. As it is, a brief general description of the reports must suffice. Almost every student subjected to this type of report has changed his opinions or at least has recognized the necessity for rethinking the whole problem under consideration. A few of the better students have even gone so far as to modify or give up entirely a few of their most cherished prejudices. They have become in some measure "creative thinkers." Furthermore, a majority of the students have shown noticeable improvements in reading and writing—especially the latter. Since no direct teaching of reading or writing skills is emphasized in this type of report, the improvements must derive from increased motivation and clarification of objectives. The students are challenged on their own ground; and, perhaps more important, they are forced to accept the challenge.

Except for a quite lengthy concluding sentence, which I find even more embarrassing than some of those I have included, this is the entire article. And I think it shows, or at least suggests, how thorough and how relentless I was in my efforts to jar the students out of their "unthinking complacency." What it doesn't show or perhaps even suggest is the fact that my efforts to jar the students were never, even in my very first classes, patronizing or unfeeling; and as the semesters rolled by, and I began to get some sense of how deeply the students' stereotypes were embedded in their minds, I became more and more sympathetic to even their feeblest attempts at "creative thinking." Then, as I became more sympathetic, the students became more trusting and consequently more responsive—until, by the end of my third year at Miami, I was, in discussing the non-fictional writings, having classes that at times fulfilled my highest expectations. Although I still had not learned how to teach fiction, or, for that matter, either poetry or drama, my success with the non-fiction was sufficient to convince me that becoming a member of an intellectual community was not my only reason for wanting to be in a university. I also knew that I wanted to teach there.

And my own subjective feelings were everywhere confirmed by the English department and the University. Despite all the difficulties I encountered outside the classroom and the department—difficulties I shall discuss presently—I could hardly have enjoyed a more idyllic apprenticeship.

iv

During my first year at Miami my personal life was also idyllic, or at least as idyllic as it could very well be—with the war and the draft and my having registered as a non-religious conscientious objector. Then came Pearl Harbor, and in a matter of days my life turned into a nightmare. Almost immediately I was reclassified 1-A, and when I appealed that classification on conscientious grounds, I was, for the better part of a year, subjected to an FBI investigation that would have done credit to the KGB. At Miami I had an FBI man peeking into my bedroom window, ransacking my office, and then, for days afterwards, questioning my neighbors, my colleagues, my friends, and even my students. And that was only the beginning. Still other FBI men soon began retracing every step I had ever taken, questioning everyone I had ever known, from my mother and stepfather to my professors at Duke and Harvard.

That the FBI should go to such lengths made no sense to me whatsoever until I began to realize that their ostensible aim—to determine whether or not I was a sincere objector—had ceased to be their real aim; that their real aim was to prove me a Communist masquerading as an objector. And they had few if any scruples in the way they went about securing their evidence, as demonstrated by the way in which they tricked my stepfather, who didn't know the difference between Moscow Reds and Cincinnati Reds, into declaring me a member of the Communist Party. The trick, I should add, lay in the FBI man's suggesting to my stepfather, who wanted to help me in any way he could, that my being a Party member would tend to prove the sincerity of my conscientious objection. Nor was my stepfather the only one so naive or misinformed. The FBI found at least two others. So when I came up for a hearing on my appeal the examining officer (the state attorney general, if I recall correctly) prefaced his interrogation by informing me that the FBI had secured three sworn statements declaring me a card-carrying Communist. Still another tactic, as it turned out. For when I said, in reply, that the statements were absurd, that I could easily disprove them, the officer acknowledged that he knew I could, that the FBI had checked them out and found them groundless. Somewhat gratified, I went on to ask him what they were going to do with the three statements—to which he replied, without batting an eye, "We're going to keep them in case we ever need them."

Except for these ominous words, which would return to haunt me years later, the hearing went very well, and I was, in fact, granted my CO status a short time afterwards. But the FBI, in the process of exonerating me officially, had visited upon me another form of condemnation. Even if their tactics had been above reproach their investigation would have tended to stir up all kinds of resentment. (In those days people resented any healthy-looking young male who wasn't in uniform.) As for me, with the FBI, in effect, suggesting that I might well be a Communist as well as a non-religious conscientious objector, I was fortunate to escape with my life. For there were efforts to poison my dog, burn down my house, and, from Georgetown, my old home-town, the threat that if I ever set foot in the town again I would be tarred and feathered and ridden out of town on a rail.

This threat brought me full circle. For all my idealism I was beginning to see the world (apart from the university) as a bigger Georgetown, inhabited by bigger scoutmasters and school principals. And my experiences with the actual draft, as a non-religious objector, provided still further confirmation. What I went through at the induction center in Cincinnati (all CO's had to go through induction, just like other draftees) would, if presented in full detail, read like a chapter out of one of Celine's novels—a chapter in which the protagonist, after being stripped and left shivering in a big hall, along with some eighty other draftees, has to step forward (while the other draftees hiss their hatred) and be branded by having a huge CO stamped on the back of his hand in red ink. Then, after one of his fellow draftees has tripped him, while another one hits him in the back and sends him flat on his face, he has to pick himself up and make his way to the first table, where he meets a serviceman who greets him with the question: "What's your religion, bud?" And when the protagonist answers, "No religion," the serviceman first explodes in a four-letter diatribe, then sends him on his way with the admonition that he'd better hide that red hand. Otherwise he may not make it through in one piece.

Needless to say I was the protagonist, and I very nearly didn't make it through in one piece. For the abuse not only continued, it soon became physical as well as verbal (*e.g.*, I never knew, till then, what a really strong shove on the back of your neck, just when you are about to have a chest X-ray, can do to your Adam's apple). And when I could stand no more and finally resisted, after being called a yellow bastard by an officer, the pent-up violence really exploded—as a half-dozen or so of the servicemen ganged up on me. They had to attack me, they later explained, because I was attacking an officer. Then, not knowing what else to do with me apparently, they carried me, groggy and half conscious, to the office of the commanding officer, who, luckily for me, turned out to be an M.D. as well as a colonel, and, more important still, a humane man. I should add that he was also a courageous man, for he took it upon himself to cut through official procedures and set me free—on the spot—by first having me declared psychoneurotic and then giving me a 4-F classification.

The colonel did, however, attach one proviso to his granting my 4-F status in the form of a stipulation that I consult a psychiatrist. Not just any psychiatrist, but one whom he specified. The colonel's intentions were certainly good; indeed, if I recall my conversation with him correctly, he even agreed to pay for my initial consultation with the psychiatrist. But the consultation itself proved farcical. The first question the psychiatrist asked me, once I had introduced myself, was a question I had already been asked, in one form or another, a hundred times over: "What would I do if a Jap parachutist came down and started raping my wife?" By way of answer I proceeded to explain, as I had done so many times before in talking to friends, and questioners, that I would try to dissuade the "Jap," that if I couldn't dissuade him I might, as a last resort, try to kill him. Then, anticipating the psychiatrist's shocked reaction, I quickly went on to explain that I did not see any inconsistency in my position, since it was one thing to kill a man who was committing rape or mayhem on me or someone dear to me and quite another to become a member of a group organized for the sole purpose of killing everyone labelled the enemy. But whatever the validity of the distinction I was drawing (and I still believe it to be perfectly valid) the psychiatrist was in no shape to recognize it. By the time I had finished my explanation he was livid with rage; and in the discussion that followed, completely abandoning his professional poise, he accused me of everything from cowardice to idiocy, the kind of idiocy being expressed in *The Nation* and *The New Republic*. And so I had no choice but to get out of the psychiatrist's office as best I could, never to return.

In citing this episode my intention is not to discredit psychiatrists, or even this psychiatrist, who in other circumstances would no doubt have proved himself quite competent. No, my intention is rather to show the incendiary effects my particular form of conscientious objection was having at that time on most everyone I encountered outside the university. Hardly anyone, it seemed, could accept my distinction between personal defense and organized killing, and those who could were as often as not upset by the way in which I presented myself and my ideas. In those days people generally demanded that a pacifist be either religious or apologetic or both. And I was neither. Consequently I just didn't fit their notion of what a pacifist should be like; I just didn't give off the right vibrations.

Toward those CO's who did, toward those who were religious, most people showed understanding, even sympathy. Warren Staebler, a colleague of mine at Miami who took the

CO position at about the same time I did, had no bad experiences of any kind, or at least none that I recall his telling me
about. He went through the same procedures, even the same induction center I went through, without a serious hitch anywhere along the line. But he was a Quaker, and a deeply religious man, whereas I was entirely on my own, with no religious
affiliations or beliefs whatsoever.

                              v

     While I made every effort to keep my pacifist ordeals entire-
ly separate from my teaching, some of my troubles as a CO
inevitably became known to my students. And I must admit
that I lived in constant fear of student reprisals; more specifically the fear that the students might succumb to the war hysteria
that was all around them and turn on me the way the psychiatrist had done. For a time, indeed, my fears and apprehensions
had me so overwrought that I mistook routine happenings for
ominous portents. On one occasion, for example, when only
two or three students out of some thirty showed up for one of
my late afternoon classes, I immediately jumped to the conclusion that the students were boycotting my class. This is it, I
thought, without even considering the possibility that they
might have other and quite different reasons for not being
there—as, in fact, they did, since the University had for some
reason or another which I did not know about at the time can-
celled all late afternoon classes on that particular day. Thanks
to this and other such instances in which my fears proved
groundless I gradually came to have more and more confidence
in the students' resistance to the hysteria of the time—a confidence that I never had reason to regret, for in all my three years
at Miami I never once experienced so much as a hint of student
disapproval that stemmed from my being a CO.
     As for the rest of the University everyone from my fellow
instructors right up to Dean Alderman and President Upham
showed me the utmost consideration. On one occasion, when I

was holding out against purchasing a war bond, and thereby preventing the University from flying the special flag that institutions could fly when all their employees had agreed to purchase bonds, three senior professors called on me—not to pressure me, or at least not to pressure me in the ordinary sense, but to try to convince me that I should, in good conscience, be willing to sign up. Or if I couldn't do that, they argued, maybe I could stretch my conscience a bit and let them buy a bond in my name—so the University could have its flag. That I could refuse this latter request now seems to me incredibly self-righteous. Yet I did refuse, politely and even regretfully but nevertheless firmly. And what now seems to me equally incredible: no one ever, to the best of my knowledge, held my refusal against me.

The one time that President Upham, himself a former English professor, called me to account had nothing to do with my being a CO or my being charged with being a Communist. Or at least his calling me to account had nothing directly to do with my being so charged. On all those serious matters he had stood behind me. What he could not countenance, or at least what he said he would not countenance, was the position I took in relation to a foolish predicament that I found myself in. The predicament derived primarily from the fact that I had become varsity tennis coach during my second year at Miami, and through my coaching had come to know a number of fraternity men, including several Sigma Nu's, who somehow got the notion that I would make an excellent advisor to their fraternity, even though I had neither been a Sigma Nu nor had anything to do with fraternities. I refused; they refused to accept my refusal. Then somehow President Upham heard and decided to intervene. He called me in to tell me that I had no choice; that if the Sigma Nu's wanted me as their advisor I would have to accept; that I might refuse military service but not, at Miami, fraternity service.

Whether President Upham was entirely serious or not I shall never know. Although I'm inclined to think he wasn't, perhaps he really was. Perhaps he believed that by forcing me to accept the advisorship he would be whipping me into more acceptable academic shape. In any event, however, I wasn't too concerned because I had already decided to go to Cornell to finish my Ph.D. Professor Simmons, with whom I had studied at Harvard, had gone to Cornell as chairman of the Slavic department and professor of English, and with his help I had secured a TA-ship that later turned into a part-time instructorship in the ASTP (Army English) program at Cornell. I hated to leave Miami, and in fact I left with the understanding that, once I had completed my Ph.D., I might return. Yet I'm not sure I ever thought I would. My friend John Weigel had already laid claim to the one course that Miami then offered in the English novel, the course I wanted to teach most, and at Miami in those days there was very little room for new courses of any kind. Then too I was becoming a bit restless, intellectually restless. I wanted to complete my Ph.D. at Cornell, but more than that I wanted to experience again the kind of intellectual stimulation I had found at Harvard.

Yet I still saw Miami as a heavenly city. My three years there had pretty much erased my unhappy experiences at Duke, which now seemed more closely linked to the FBI and the draft than to the enlightened world I had been teaching in. Of course I knew that the bigger Georgetown (the world of the draft and the FBI) was still there, that this world is in fact what we usually call the real world, and that neither I nor anyone else could ever escape from it altogether, but I also knew that I had found in the academic world, the world which we usually refer to as an ivory tower, a place in which I could live and develop without giving in to the so-called real. More important still, I knew that I wanted to teach in this world as well as live in it, and thus give others the chance to live and develop. And if I had not as yet mastered the art of teaching, as I conceived of teaching, I felt confident that I could eventually do so.

3

My Apprenticeship Continued at Cornell and Harvard and Berkeley

W HEN I arrived in Ithaca for the summer session of 1943 I was disappointed to find that neither Professor Simmons nor Professor Brown, the only people whom I knew at Cornell, would be around until late August or early September. But I didn't worry too much. I merely reported to the acting chairman, whose name is no longer consequential here, to secure what I supposed would be his routine approval for the tentative program I had already worked out with Professors Brown and Simmons—a program in which I would be spending the next eight or nine months preparing for my orals, which I would take some time during the spring semester.

At this point, for those not acquainted with the old-fashioned "Doctors Orals," I must explain that these were oral examinations in which anywhere from eight to ten professors (representing the various periods and types of English literature from *Beowulf* to Hardy) took turns questioning the candidate on his knowledge and critical understanding. The common though not invariable practice was for each professor to begin with some ridiculously easy question, then to proceed to more and more difficult questions until the candidate broke down (*i.e.*, could no longer answer). So that by the end of the usual two-and-a-half to three hours (my exam went longer) the candidate had been broken down some eight or ten times, and was, as often as not, on the verge of nervous collapse. For the exam, as the candidate knew all too well, would pretty much determine his fate for the rest of his academic life. True, he might possibly get another chance, but even if he passed the second time he would still carry the stigma of his original failure. The exam, then, was a terrifying ordeal in itself, and since most graduate students began preparing a semester or two before they took the actual exam, the ordeal really lasted for the better part of a year—in some cases even longer.

I mention all this for several reasons, the first being to convey some sense of how completely I was taken aback when the acting chairman, after looking over my tentative program, wanted to know why I was postponing my orals. After all, he pointed out, I had already completed two years of course work in two reputable universities, and should now be coming up for my orals. At this point, unable to believe he was saying what he seemed to be saying, I rather lamely asked what he meant by "now"—to which he replied, after looking at his calendar, "a week from this coming Thursday." By this time I knew that something strange was going on, but rather than fight him or it, I said a week from Thursday would be fine, that I would see him then. (The something strange that was going on, I eventually learned, had to do with my being a protege of E. J. Simmons, and with there being considerable resistance in the English department to his coming to Cornell as Professor of English as well as chairman of Slavic).

Why I chose not to resist an act so grotesquely unjust I still do not know for sure. Perhaps, remembering the trouble I had got myself into at Duke, I felt that Cornell was my last chance for a Ph.D. and I had better begin by trying to do what I was told. Or perhaps I sensed that I had everything to gain and nothing to lose; that if I failed in such bizarre circumstances my failure could hardly be held against me; that if, on the other hand, I somehow managed to pass, I would escape agonizing months of preparation and be home free. Which is how it finally turned out. After reading Legouis and Cazamian's *History of English Literature* for ten consecutive days I went to the exam, met my examiners for the first time, and proceeded to answer their questions, as best I could, for almost four hours. (The longer the exams went, after two-and-a-half hours, the worse you were doing). Then, after I had waited outside the examination room for another forty-five minutes (the longer you had to wait the worse you had done) Professor William Sale, Jr. emerged, put his arm around my shoulder, and said, "Well, son, you didn't exactly bowl them over in there, but you passed, and that's all that matters." And that's all that did matter: I had lucked out once again.

By thus slipping through the ordeal intended to separate the qualified from the unqualified among doctoral candidates I had, in effect, become one of the qualified without ever having been really tested, without ever having been obliged to toe the academic line, and, perhaps even more important, without ever having really suffered. Professor Baum, like so many academics a great believer in suffering as well as toeing the line, would have been completely aghast. After what he had threatened me with in my upcoming orals at Duke, as a way of trying to whip me into proper academic shape, he would have viewed my Cornell orals as a minor academic disaster, as a case in which a great university had, through inadvertence, permitted a man who had not yet learned the rudiments of academic discipline to become a candidate for its highest degree. And of course he would have been, in his own terms, quite right. The most terrifying ordeal that the academic system imposes had not, thanks to my incredible good fortune, been an ordeal at all: my orals had neither disciplined me nor shaped me; they had not even seriously affected me.

ii.

Of course I still had to complete my dissertation, a monumental task in those days when it was expected that dissertations would be significant contributions to knowledge. Yet somehow I did not find the prospect of two or more years of research and writing, in the time I could steal from teaching, to be especially daunting, perhaps because I had already discussed a possible subject with Professor Simmons, a study of Charles Reade as a sociological novelist that I knew I would find interesting. The study I had in mind could, I realized, be controversial, since I planned to draw upon Marxist critical theory, but with Professor Simmons' backing I did not foresee any serious difficulties. Nor were there any.

While my research took longer than I expected, that was in part because I put aside the dissertation at times to publish three quite long scholarly articles on Charles Reade (in *PMLA*, *American Literature*, and *Studies in Philology*). For me or anyone to publish in this way now, in the present academic climate, would certainly bespeak ambition, perhaps inordinate ambition. Like that of a graduate student I had some years ago who didn't want to write a seminar paper more than fifteen typed pages long because—and he said all this with a straight face—he would be reducing his chances of getting a term paper published as an article, since most scholarly journals were no longer accepting articles longer than fifteen pages. Quite possibly there were a few graduate students as nutty as this in the forties, although I have my doubts. While "publish or perish" had already gone into effect in many leading universities it had not as yet taken the virulent forms it has taken in the past twenty or twenty-five years. In any case I had little if any sense that publication was a means of getting ahead in the academic world. There had been no such emphasis at Miami, nor, for that matter, in any form that I took seriously, at Duke or Harvard or Cornell. Professor Sale, who became my good friend and mentor at Cornell, as well as my advisor, did not urge me to publish. Neither did Professor Simmons, although he himself published widely. I did it, not out of ambition, but out of sheer naive scholarly enthusiasm.

At this juncture it may seem as if I am protesting too much. Why, it may be asked, can't I admit to a bit of ambition? What's wrong with ambition? Or getting ahead? To which I have to answer: there's nothing wrong, if you're in business, or selling cars, or engaged in any activity which has as its end money or power. If I had been doing any of these things I would have been ambitious too. But teaching, as I conceived of it (and still do), could admit no such ends, or means. If I had been publishing to get ahead I would have been playing an academic game—the game that, for academics, is played for the very highest stakes in terms of power, prestige, and money. And in playing that game I would have been accepting the worst side of the prevailing academic system: I would have been agreeing to turn out reviews and books and articles for the sake of promotions, and yes, even merit raises. In other words I would have turned myself into what used to be called a literary hack, and in the process would have emasculated myself as both a writer and teacher. No hack could teach literature the way I was teaching it: he couldn't even want to. He would have seen what I was attempting as too naive, or too idealistic, or too personal, or too unprofessional, or too scary.

iii

During the time I was at Cornell, however, I had another and different version of the academic system to contend with in my teaching—in the form of ASTP or Army English. Given a choice I would never have taught in the ASTP program, but if I was going to teach at all I had no alternative, since the traditional courses in Freshman Comp as well as the V5 or V7 Navy courses (which were in all essentials traditional courses limited to navy men) had, understandably enough, been pre-empted by the faculty. While a few professors chose to teach ASTP English out of a sense of patriotic duty, some 80 percent of the courses, I would estimate, were assigned to TA's and part-time instructors.

My own reluctance to teach in the program, I should explain, had little if anything to do with my principles, which were of course anti-war but not Quixotically absolutist. (Whomever or whatever I taught I would, I believed, be contributing to the war effort.) No, what scared me was having anything whatsoever to do with the army. After my experiences in the induction center I wasn't at all sure that servicemen, and more especially the older ones who had already seen action overseas, would be able to tolerate my being a CO. Seemingly I could have hidden my conscientious objections, and I might have attempted to do just that if I had thought myself capable of suppressing my anti-war sentiments and ideas. But I knew I couldn't: I knew that sooner or later in my classes I would speak out in ways that would betray my attitudes; and I also knew, or sensed, that the men in my classes would be more likely to tolerate my views if they knew how seriously I held them.

On both counts, as it turned out, I was right. In the very first minute of my very first ASTP class I gave myself away, at least partially, when I expressed complete dismay at the way in which the class stood at attention while two of its members marched from the back of the room forward, finally to stop in front of my desk, give a smart salute, then hand me two copies of the class roll. While some of the instructors actually learned to return the salute, as we were apparently expected to do, I never could. For that matter I never could learn to take the ASTP seriously in any of its military postures. I tried, but I just couldn't manage it.

Yet the students, who were, as I recall, referred to as cadets, didn't seem to be the least bit upset by my unmilitary responses. If anything they seemed to be relieved to find someone who wasn't taken in by the military antics they were obliged to go through. For the whole ASTP program at Cornell was absurdly ill-conceived, however one looked at it. The men were shoved into the program on the basis of tests, without regard for their own wishes in the matter; then they were obliged to live in barracks (as if they were still in basic training) and march to class with backpacks and in formation, while navy students, in the quite sensible navy program, would be lolling around on the grass with their girlfriends. On occasion the navy men would even jeer as the hapless cadets marched by. And to make matters still more unpleasant for the cadets they were constantly being told, by many of their patriotic instructors, how lucky they were to be in the ASTP and how serious were the obligations they had to fulfill. While these exhortations were doubtless sincere and well intentioned, the cadets understandably found them irritating—in at least one instance so irritating that they actually turned on the instructor, a professor in the speech department, and not only ran him out of the classroom but forced him to take refuge behind the locked door of his office.

With the cadets in such a defiant mood—and they were more or less in this mood the whole time I was there—my unmilitary posture hardly proved to be a handicap in the classroom. Nor were they put off by my attempts to deal logically and critically with whatever came up in the class discussion—without regard for its patriotic or military implications. Actually the texts we used, together with the syllabuses we were supposed to follow, left very few openings for any kind of free thinking, but I did what I could—and the cadets responded quite favorably. At one point, when it seemed as if the whole English portion of the program might be on the verge of collapse, I was asked if I would be willing to serve as a kind of unofficial chairman and try to get a group of instructors together who could get along with the cadets. I think perhaps I found the proposal flattering. Or if I didn't I should have since it would be the only time I would be asked to be chairman of anything.

Nevertheless I knew I could not accept. To do so, I felt, would be to desert the students and go over to the side of their oppressors—Cornell and the army, or more specifically, Cornell acting as an agent for the army. Perhaps it took this kind of situation, with the university representing the army, to make me realize that I, as a teacher, had obligations which took precedence over my obligation to the university as an institution. Up to this point in my teaching career, because of my idyllic apprenticeship at Miami, I had been trying to see myself as a member of a department as well as an individual teacher. But the way things worked out at Cornell I more and more came to see myself as an individual teacher aligned with the students against the ASTP and the department. And so, without fully realizing what I was doing, I had begun to cut the basic ties that bind most professors to one another and to their departments and their profession. These can, I acknowledge, be honorable ties. Some of the best teachers I have known over the years (including one of my closest friends, the late Professor Edward E. Bostetter) have subscribed to them. But for me the ties were crippling. If I was going to teach the way I wanted to teach I had to break them, and, on the positive side, I had to continue to align myself with the students.

iv

Luckily for me my next teaching job was at Harvard (in Theodore Morrison's English A division of the English department), where everything was so wide open that I could indulge my individual and anti-departmental proclivities to the full. In fact the way Professor Morrison ran the department it was not so much a department as a collection of sometimes strange and mostly gifted individuals exercising their individuality in the teaching of literature and composition. There were some rules, of course, about writing assignments and conference hours, but few if any of the usual departmental demands or pressures. In my own case, for example, Professor Morrison had apparently been warned, just before he hired me, that I wasn't altogether safe, that I might get into trouble. A fair enough warning, everything considered, yet it failed to deter Professor Morrison, who is said to have answered: "I can get a hundred men who won't do anything wrong. Give me someone who may do something right, and I'll put up with his doing a few things wrong."

Quite possibly I used up my quota of wrongs, although I don't think any of them proved embarrassing to Professor Morrison or the department, save perhaps my run-in with Father Feeney, a Cambridge priest, over the way I was teaching Voltaire; and even that could hardly have been taken too seriously, since Father Feeney was not only notorious for his witch-hunting but actually managed to get himself excommunicated a few years later. On the positive side I think much of what I did was, in Professor Morrison's loose departmental terms, right. Certainly it was, from first to last, right for me. I had only three classes (two at Harvard, one at Radcliffe), with some eighteen to twenty students in each, meeting twice a week. As for the students themselves, they ranged from intelligent to brilliant, with a good percentage of my two classes at Harvard made up of returning veterans. What we did in the courses was in large measure up to me: in English A, it's true, every instructor had to use a certain anthology and assign a certain amount of writing, but the anthology (*Five Kinds of Writing*) was wonderfully rich, the writing assignments flexible. And English B, which was even more wide open, I turned into an introduction to drama and fiction, with Voltaire's *Tales*, Hardy's *Jude the Obscure* and Shaw's *Man and Superman* as my texts.

For the kind of teaching I wanted to do at that point there could hardly have been a more perfect set-up, and in the months that followed I made the most of my opportunities—to teach as I had never taught before. It wasn't that I was doing anything different or better in my teaching, at least not as far as I could tell; it was the students, and perhaps the time and place (Harvard in the first year after the war) or in any case some different and seemingly magical ingredients in the situation. Everything that came up in class seemed to be as exciting to the students as to me. In English A, for example, I somehow managed to introduce, of all the books I might have chosen for extra reading, Carlyle's *Sartor Resartus*—perhaps, for students, the most unreadable of all nineteenth-century books, if I may judge by my later experiences here at Washington in teaching courses in nineteenth-century prose. Yet it proved to be a huge success in English A—in part, no doubt, because of the fairly sensational parallels I tried to draw in class between Carlyle and Hitler, and more especially between Carlyle's prose and Hitler's speeches. Yet if I provided the spark, that was all I did. It was the students themselves who took fire. The proof is that I drew the same or at least similar parallels in my later classes and they invariably fell rather flat.

Nor can I take very much credit as a teacher for what happened in English B. I still hadn't learned to teach fiction. The ASTP classes at Cornell had included very little creative literature of any kind; and while Professor Sale had, from time to time, permitted me to give lectures in his courses in the modern American novel, in order to give me experience in lecturing to a class of 150 students, I did not, and still do not, consider lecturing to be teaching. What I had been looking for, and had not yet found, were some reasonably sure ways to help the students connect Voltaire and Hardy and Shaw with their own lives. But the students were so perceptive that my continuing uncertainty didn't really matter. They not only found ways on their own, they showed me how to find them.

Jude the Obscure, as might be expected, elicited the most powerful responses. When we first started talking about this novel in class one student, a quite tall and ungainly young man named Pond, became so upset that he actually jumped up and paced back and forth at the side of our classroom. Then, a few evenings later, while I was sitting in my office on the top floor of an old frame building called Warren House, I heard a tremendous racket and bellowing on the stairs, as if a bull were loose in the stairwell. Just a few seconds later a book came flying through my door and by my head, and the tall young man himself appeared, asking how in God's name I could assign such an awful book. At that point I presumed the book was *Jude*, although I didn't have a clue as to what he had found so objectionable until he mentioned the hanging of the children. Now I'm not trying to suggest that having a somewhat mixed up student throw a book at my head as he burst into my office constituted the ultimate literary response. But I knew for sure that the student had achieved a powerful connection.

Then, a few days later, I encountered a connection even more powerful, this time on the part of a girl in my Radcliffe class who made a special appointment to talk with me about *Jude*, only to find herself unable to speak. After we sat for about forty-five minutes in virtual silence I asked her if she would like to return the next day—to try again. She returned; we sat for another hour or so; then she blurted out: "I know that Sue (the heroine of *Jude*) is a Lesbian; I know she is because I am." At this point a more cautious teacher (or perhaps I should say a more responsible and professional one) would have stopped the girl right there and suggested that she see the school psychiatrist. And I must admit that I was tempted to do so, as I had been tempted on a few less scary occasions while I was teaching at Miami. Yet I didn't stop her because I was beginning to realize that the kind of reading I was trying to get the students to do would, if it were successful, inevitably provoke such responses; that if I were going to teach novels this way I was going to have to expect extreme and/or mixed up responses; that there was no way the extreme and mixed up could be separated, *a priori*, from the original and the perceptive.

I don't mean to suggest that I had all this worked out in consistent intellectual terms. For one thing I had not yet read D. H. Lawrence seriously, had not yet comprehended his critical argument to the effect that all art, if it is genuine, is going to "hurt." No, I was just groping my way towards an understanding of what was going on in my classes, as one student's reactions to some character, scene, or episode in *Jude* gave rise to still other reactions, other comments—finally to reveal to me, as well as to the participating students themselves, a far richer novel than I had been able to realize through my own reading, even though, in my own reading I had drawn upon a considerable body of published criticism.

In the process of teaching *Jude* to these classes I had, more or less unwittingly, gone far beyond my original intention, which was to try to get the students to experience the novel as I had experienced it. In trying to do that I had pushed the students, or they had pushed themselves, far beyond my own perceptions, and I was learning from them as well as they from me. How fully I understood the ramifications of this discovery I am not at all sure, although I do feel certain that I had some sense of where it might be taking me. Certainly I knew, and it was truly exhilarating to know, that every time I entered the classroom I was embarking on an uncharted intellectual voyage, with not much more than a compass to steer by; and I think I also knew that we might end up on the rocks but that, if we came through, as, luckily, we always managed to do, we would be somewhere neither I nor they had ever been before. While all this may, I realize, sound romantic, or at least drastically overstated, I don't believe it is. I remember too clearly the way I couldn't sleep the nights before I met the classes, not because I was anxious or upset, but because I was so keyed up over where we might be going in class the next day.

v

How I could give up this teaching and Harvard to go to Berkeley I shall never fully understand, perhaps because, for the first (and I hope the last) time in my life I went completely against my wishes and feelings and instincts and tried to act wholly on the basis of what I thought was sound academic advice. But there were irrational elements that the rational advice could hardly account for, beginning with my very first meeting with B. H. Lehman, the chairman of the department at Berkeley. I was attending the MLA convention of 1944, and because a friend of mine with whom I was going to have lunch had lined up for a brief interview with the Berkeley chairman, I thought I might as well get in line too. At the time I had no serious thoughts about Berkeley; I'm not even sure I knew about its academic reputation. Nor was I much impressed with Lehman, who struck me as being some strange kind of academic huckster, with his talk of "windows on the sea" and "straight lines through to the full professorship" (talk that some of the younger men in the department at Berkeley called Lehmanese). During the interview, therefore, I was quite offhand, and when it was over, and I said good-bye to Lehman, I hadn't the slightest notion that I would hear from him again. But something about me, something I said or did, apparently caused him to form a completely erroneous impression of me, caused him to see me as having the makings of a scholar-clubman, his ideal conception of what a Berkeley professor should be. So I not only heard from him a month or two later, he actually went on to offer me a job for the coming year, contingent upon a California law against former CO's being rescinded by that time—a law which held that no one who had been a CO in World War II could hold any kind of state-funded position in California. As it happened, the law was not rescinded in time, although Lehman assured me it soon would be, and that he would renew his offer of an appointment as soon as possible—for 1946.

Needless to say, he did renew his offer, in phrases so glowing that I found them difficult to resist. As for my friends and advisors at Harvard, they couldn't understand how I could hesitate, even for a moment. It was, they argued, the chance of a lifetime, a chance to develop and mature and have classes of my own, whereas my appointment at Harvard was, in their view, a dead end. And they didn't mince words in letting me know how dead the end might be: "You'll be maybe five or six more years, and then *finis*. Harry Levin, the only man who ever went from English A to a tenured position, accomplished that feat years ago. The way things are now someone at Podunk College would have a better chance of securing an associate professorship at Harvard than someone who is actually here." All this I understood, insofar as I could understand such things at that time. Yet I still wanted to stay. If I could have five more years like the one I was enjoying why not take them. Then I could start worrying about my academic future.

While Professor Morrison sympathized with my wish to stay, he too insisted that I had no choice but to accept Lehman's offer. And when I still seemed reluctant to leave, he arranged for me to have a talk with Professor Douglas Bush, to see what my chances for staying on at Harvard might be if I remained in English A. By this time I suspected that I was, for my own good, being shoved out of Harvard and sent to California. Yet I hardly expected Bush to be so vehement in his dismissal. Apparently the way I talked about scholarship and teaching, the way Lehman had found so promising, had just the opposite effect on Bush. He became more and more hostile, the longer we talked, finally to end up telling me I would be "a viper in the bosom of any English department."

I can see now that Bush understood me far better than Lehman. At the time, however, his words had little effect. Because of the success I had enjoyed in my teaching I still did not realize how far I had strayed from the accepted principles and practices of nearly all English departments. Consequently, I still did not know, and apparently my friends and well-wishers did not know (although Professor Bush did), that I could not possibly fit into the Berkeley department. And since I did not and could not know, I went.

vi

For all my reluctance, all my doubts, I arrived in Berkeley feeling reasonably hopeful. But I had not been in Wheeler Hall (where the English department then had its offices) more than a few hours before I began to wonder what I had got myself into, beginning with the fact that I had to share a tiny office, hardly big enough for one, with a full professor who proceeded to explain, with incredible naivete, I thought, that he would be my big brother for the next year or so. While he didn't actually refer to himself as "big brother" his meaning became clear enough when he set about fulfilling his role—as if I were a newly pledged member of some grand and sophisticated fraternity, or, more accurately, I suppose, as if I were a young scholar-clubman being introduced to the customs and rules of the club. When it was time to go to lunch, for example, my big brother informed me that we were expected to have lunch at the Faculty Club, at the English table. He even tried, at the actual lunch, to show me, through his own example, how I might take part in the epigrammatic exchanges. I know that's what he was doing because, on the way back to Wheeler, he made everything explicit.

At this point, somewhat dismayed, I tried to take refuge in the possibility that I had just happened to draw an overly-zealous big brother. But I could no longer hold onto that possibility when I began to encounter attitudes much like his all over the place. If I said something about the weather, my remarks would apparently be weighed to see if I really was unhappy with the climate (which of course I wasn't). If I said something about the cover of my copy of *Partisan Review* having been mangled in the mail, the next thing I knew Lehman or someone else would be trying to justify the mails on the West Coast. If I failed to look impressed by someone's Latin quotation (at lunch, or in the hallway) someone would be sure to ask me whether or not I had the highest regard for such performances.

I don't mean to be unfair. Attitudes such as this exist in all departments, I'm sure, though perhaps not in what I would be inclined to characterize as such neurotic form. It's even possible that Lehman fostered these attitudes, in part at least, in an effort to be fair, to let new people know what was expected of them. Certainly Lehman went out of his way, in my case, to let me know what his expectations were. More than once during my first semester at Berkeley he stopped by to take me to lunch at the Black Sheep, a quiet little restaurant on the Avenue, where he would go into considerable detail about what he called my "refusal to accept the greatness that was being thrust upon me." Then, by way of partially defining "greatness" in relation to teaching, he would declare, "Better to stand within a hundred yards of a great man than sit at the feet of a mediocre one." (Lehmanese was closely related to Carlylese). Then, on one occasion, when I was pressing him for a closer definition of greatness, he actually said that it had been conferred upon me by my having been chosen to come to Berkeley, that all I had to do, once again, was accept it: "You have so much charm, Wayne," he would say, "why do you have to waste it on students?" Or: "If you talk to a graduate student more than five minutes you're wiping his nose"—a statement which clearly implied that you didn't talk to undergraduates at all, if there were any way to avoid it.

I hope it doesn't seem as if I am belatedly trying to get Lehman. Actually, as I came to know him better, I couldn't help liking him as a man. I might even have put up with his ideas and attitudes, appalling as I found them, if they had been his alone. But they weren't. He had, in large measure, recreated the department in his own image. Certain professors, it is true, did not actively conform to the image. Mark Schorer and Gordon McKenzie, for example. Yet they acquiesced in it. Even as they would say something like, "Oh, that's just Ben Lehman," as if they were dismissing him or patronizing him, they were really kidding themselves, because Ben's ways and Ben's values prevailed. If I spent time talking to a student Ben would somehow hear about it and remind me that my time might be better spent on an article for *PMLA*. Or if I had coffee with an undergraduate girl Ben would hear about that and wag his finger and say, "You understand, Wayne, you're not to seduce the undergraduates." And when I simply refused to give a reading—everyone in the department was supposed to give some kind of reading (usually from some well-known poetic or dramatic work) for the students and the general public once during the school year—everyone seemed almost as upset as Lehman. Not that very many of them wished to give such a reading. It was just that Lehman, who was himself a consummate showman and lecturer and thrived on such performances, had convinced them that it was their duty to follow his lead.

During my first semester at Berkeley about the only person on the faculty I could talk to at all frankly was Roy Harvey Pearce, who was, if I recall correctly, the only other new man in the department that year. Roy and I became really good friends, and even though my views were not Roy's by any means, we did, I think, give each other considerable moral support. But for me it wasn't enough. Once again, as in the past, I began to find the students more congenial and interesting than my colleagues—a tendency that Lehman (once he had given up on me, as he pretty much had, I believe, by the end of the first semester) actively fostered by appointing me advisor to the writers' group connected with the University—a group that included Robert

Duncan, Jack Spicer, and many other poets who made up what was then called the Berkeley Renaissance and later became the nucleus of the Beat movement.

By this time, by the end of my first year, I knew for sure that I was through at Berkeley. Really, I suppose, I had known it at the end of the first week, perhaps even the first day. I knew that I could no more become the scholar-clubman that Lehman and the department wanted than I could become an executive in a department store—a comparison that is more apt than might at first seem apparent, for executive ability was another facet of the scholar-clubman that Lehman much prized. As well he might, for the classes were, wherever and whenever possible, kept so large that they could hardly be taught without readers, who had to be directed and managed like employees. One class that I developed on my own, a senior-graduate class (limited to fifteen students), in which I attempted to combine criticism with a huge amount of critical writing, proved quite successful the first time I gave it (in the fall of '46–'47). Then, when I offered it again in the following year and something like sixty or seventy students tried to enroll, Lehman was all for letting them in and giving me a corps of five readers. By this time, however, I think he knew that I wouldn't accept, that I would refuse the call to greatness.

The teaching that I did manage to do, despite having classes of sixty in Freshman English, with a TA to read papers and confer with students, was nevertheless gratifying. In fact the two undergraduate seminars I did on Dickens (limited to fifteen students) were very nearly as exciting, and in some ways even more rewarding, than my English B class at Harvard. For one thing, these seminars gave me my first opportunity to carry through, in the classroom, a full consideration of a great writer's artistic achievement. And our scholarly and critical explorations proved all the more interesting to the students because, at that time, Dickens had not yet been revived, nor had the connections between his writings and Kafka's, which we explored in some detail, been much discussed. So it was all new and exciting, to them and to me.

vii

Once again I must add that I had not yet, to my own satisfaction, learned how to teach fiction. But the courses themselves, like all the other courses I taught at Berkeley, were remarkably successful, and since I was also continuing to publish (despite my refusal to accept any obligation to do so), Lehman would have found it a bit awkward if I had really wanted to stay on. But of course I didn't. I had already begun trying to find a way out, and back to Harvard and English A, before the end of my first semester at Berkeley. At that point, for all my dismay at what I had got myself into, I still did not feel trapped. Lehman was a nutty character, and Berkeley, as I saw it, a nutty place, but there were other departments in other universities, and I couldn't believe that very many of them were like Berkeley. All I would have to do would be to write to my friends back East, giving them a more complete picture of the Berkeley department than I had previously done; then they would see my predicament pretty much the way I did and help me find a job in a different kind of place.

But the answers I received, when I actually did write, took me completely aback. Sympathetic as the letters were, there was no mistaking their message: Berkeley may be bad, from your point of view, but all English departments are like that, and if you want to stay in teaching you will have to accept them for what they are and shape up accordingly. Professor Morrison, in his letter, put it this way:

Dear Wayne,

I have every sympathy with you as I know you will believe. At the same time, you yourself, no less than the University, have pretty clearly reached the conclusion that you will never really feel at home where you are.

For the kind of teaching you want to do, I hardly know what place under current conditions is going to be ideal, not, at any rate, until you have worked up the seniority ladder, and can form your own program. I don't see how you can escape being prepared to make some sacrifices of taste and preference until you reach this goal. You can continue to believe that education ought to proceed by personal and individual relations, but it may be too much to expect any actual institution to conform to this belief.

As far as English A is concerned, I have already told you that I think it would be a great mistake for you to come back here, even if I let you. The corollary is that it would be a mistake on my part to let you even if I could, and I hope that you will not think too unkindly of me for saying so. You ought to get a foot-hold where you can stay put, and work up. I wish I could be a better advisor to you. I sympathize completely with a great part of your feelings as you express them, but perhaps I ought to say frankly that I am not fully at ease about it all. I think it may well be, although, of course, this is partly guesswork, that Lehman is a little baffled, and cannot tell you at quite what points he is dis-satisfied because he doesn't know. (I only talked five minutes and very generally with Lehman, so that I am not reporting any-thing he said about you. What he said, in fact, was favorable.)

It is one thing to be critical of education generally, and of the university one works for, as many of us, for example, are very critical of Harvard. It is another to show in perhaps uninten-tional ways a sense of grievance or discomfort which suggests in-ability or malaise at working in harness. I think, myself, that education has to contain a good deal of the individual and per-sonal, and is in an unhappy state as a mass phenomenon. At the same time, I have an equally firm conviction that it is possible for an instructor to do harm by overanxious personal fostering of students. On these points, a breath of advice from me might mean something.

Professor Morrison's refusal to let me return I had more or less expected. What hit me the hardest in his letter was the way in which he so drastically misconstrued what I was trying to do in my teaching, particularly his reference to "overanxious, per-sonal fostering of students." As for his advice, it struck me as being much the same advice, however different his motives, as that I had been getting from my childhood onwards—from my high-school principal right on to Professor Baum.

Nor was Professor Simmons' advice, although I felt he was offering it in a wholly different spirit, all that different—as advice:

Dear Wayne:

I was extremely sorry to get your package of bad news from California. I have a real sympathy for your position, but I do think that you will soon have to take a thorough inventory of yourself, and your ideas, and ideals, and decide where you are heading. I am sure California is all that you say, but then I am just as sure that virtually every other major University and nearly all the colleges would present the same difficulties. If one is to stay in teaching with the kind of ideals and hopes that people like yourself and myself possess, then one must strike a fine balance between acceptance and rejection. To be sure, I taught only a single summer at California some seven years ago. I came in contact in that short time with a number of the disadvantages you mention. But I also quickly found the kind of intellectual climate, restricted, to be sure, but vigorous and interesting, that I wanted. It was a good little group of Teacher's Union people there, and though they could not work miracles, they kept up one's spirit and drive. I am sure that kind of circle still exists at California.

And this is the way it will be in every university or college, with variations in strength and weakness in the matter of this element. Harvard, in this respect, is no better and no worse than most of the other places. There does happen to be a larger progressive element there, but I should think your first experience in Cambridge would convince you that even this element can be quickly squelched the moment it is effective.

All I am trying to say is that you must make up your mind to accept most untoward conditions that you meet in our institutions of higher learning, and then do your best to work with the progressive group for changes. This is all anyone can hope to do in America, in one's own small sphere of interest, in these days.

If you do not intend to stick it out at California, I don't think you are doing wrong in going back to Harvard, if you can get in. But you must be perfectly certain that there is no future for you there and that eventually you will have to go out into the world of light—or darkness—once again.

Much as I appreciated what Professor Simmons was trying to do for me, there was no way I could see his message as anything but devastating. If he and Professor Sale, who also wrote most sympathetically, and all my other trusted advisors were right, the entire academic world took on the hues of Duke and Berkeley: the heavenly cities I had found were Quixotic mirages which I had conjured up, like the good Don himself, out of my youthful reading and my equally youthful exuberance. And now I had to grow up and adapt to the real academic world—a bigger, more sophisticated Georgetown, or in Professor Simmons' words, a world not of light, but of darkness. But I knew very well that I couldn't grow up, couldn't accept the darkness—no matter how many people advised me, no matter how hard I tried. If teaching meant moving to another Berkeley and then shaping up I would have to give up teaching altogether. It would be all over.

viii

For a considerable time, indeed right up to the time I went to the University of Washington, I did think it was all over. Various people were trying to help me in various ways, and something might have come from some of their efforts if I had been more interested. Mark Schorer, I know, explored a number of possibilities for me that I should have followed up. In writing to Bennington, for example, he even paid me the dubious compliment of being, in his words, "born to be a Bennington professor." Yet, much as I appreciated his and other such efforts, I couldn't develop any real enthusiasm for job-hunting. Not when the best I could hope for seemed to be another or lesser Berkeley.

Quite possibly my depressed state aroused genuine concern on Lehman's part; either that or he was beginning to get worried about student reaction. Even in those days the students at Berkeley were extremely volatile, and might have been incited to some kind of protest on my behalf. In any event Lehman quite early began stirring around to see if he could help. To that end he wrote an amazing letter—a letter he was kind enough to show me—in which he presented me in what were, for him, quite restrained terms:

> Burns has been with us for two years as Instructor, and factors in our local situation make it impossible to accord him the Assistant Professorship he amply deserves. He is an excellent and even a remarkable teacher. We have not now on our junior staff a man who better balances the function of insight into literature with the function of insight into growing minds. The students follow him through from course to course and, when they do not continue taking courses in the field, they come to him personally. For them, in all circumstances, he always has time. Indeed, there filter into this office reports of a considerable number of cases in which he has gone out of his way to find and help former students of his of whose need for help he had heard. In the classroom he has clarity, force, vivacity, imagination, and he does not shirk or evade rigorous discipline.
>
> With such a warranted encomium, it may well be asked why he is not awarded the Assistant Professorship here on the basis of his teaching, especially since he has, for a young man, done a good deal of publishing and has considerable projects under way. As it has happened, we need in the field of his special interest a man who will make somewhat different emphases from those that are natural to him, and we need immediately for the place that he would fill a young man of striking administrative aptitude, which Burns has not. Though we are not now finding a place for him, I should not be surprised if, in a few years, we moved into the contradictory position of urging him to return to us.

The letter didn't surprise me. Actually it was pretty much what I expected, and I thought it might be of some help, provided I could find somewhere I might want to go, and provided Lehman's encomiums, heaped as they were on top of my firing, didn't arouse all kinds of dreadful suspicions. Then I thought: What the hell? Why not arouse the suspicions? Always before, although I had never tried to sell myself, I had at least compromised with the hiring system to the point of letting my appearance and manner and words be misunderstood—if, as in the case of Lehman, someone seemed bent on misunderstanding them. But I never would again. My experiences at Berkeley had at least taught me that much. Henceforth—if there were to be a henceforth—I would insist on my viperish qualities, in case the people I talked to were, like Lehman, unable to see for themselves what had been so clear to Douglas Bush. So I had no cause to worry about suspicions. They might even provide a good starting point for any future interviews. And that, as it turned out, was how they actually functioned.

At the time I am referring to, in February or March of 1948, I had no sense of the University of Washington at all—except as its football and basketball teams played in the Pacific Coast Conference. Then I read an article of Porter G. Perrin's in *College English* which I found much to my liking, especially in what it had to say about university teaching. Here, I thought, were ideas I could live with and teach with, and I noted with some interest that Perrin had recently moved from Colgate to Washington. About the same time I also became aware of the Canwell Hearings in the state of Washington, McCarthy-type hearings which were causing liberal and radical academics everywhere to shake in their shoes—and with reason. But in my situation I was past shaking. What interested me was the fact that of the six or seven Communists or former Communists (numbers and exact affiliations weren't too clear) the Canwell Committee had presumably identified, something like four or five had been or still were in the English department at the University of Washington. A surprising number, considering the size of the English department in relation to the rest of the University, and one which further convinced me that Washington might be the place for me—not because of my own Marxist background, or at least not primarily because of that, but rather because a department which could include that many Marxists, along with Porter Perrin, must be a wide-open department indeed.

At the same time I had to recognize—and in this I had considerable help from my good friend Roy Pearce—how vulnerable I would be to the Canwell investigators. There was no telling, Roy pointed out, how long their hearings and investigations would continue. Nor was there any telling what the aftermath might be. In going to Washington, with my earlier Communist involvements a matter of FBI record, I would be putting a noose around my own neck and asking the Canwell Committee to pull. Roy's arguments gave me pause, I must admit, yet I could also see how the situation at Washington might actually work to my advantage. Who would expect anyone worried about his earlier Communist proclivities to be foolish enough to go barging into the middle of an investigation? In the circumstances Washington might, paradoxically, be the safest place for me to be.

How I proceeded, once I made up my mind that Washington was my best if not my only alternative, I am no longer certain. Nor does it matter greatly. I do know that Lehman sent a version of the letter I have quoted to Perrin, who wrote to inform me that he had sent it on to Robert B. Heilman, who was in the process of taking over the chairmanship of the department. Then, some time later, I made a formal application, accompanied by still another letter from Lehman, and Heilman invited me to come up to Seattle on June 25 for an interview with him and a talk with members of the department. Even then I was not too sanguine. For one thing, I knew Heilman only as a leading New Critic and as the author of *Introduction to Drama*, and I couldn't really believe that he would look favorably on someone as deeply and unalterably opposed to the New Criticism as I already knew myself to be.

Nevertheless I liked Heilman from the start, especially the way he got right down to the business of Lehman's phony letter. Not that he called the letter phony. He merely pointed out that if I was half as good as the letter said I was California wouldn't be letting me go, and then went on to ask me if I would like to give him the whole story. Accustomed to Lehmanese as I had become, Heilman's directness struck me as something wonderful—as if I had finally escaped from Kafka's castle into broad daylight—and I began to feel that perhaps he really could understand what I had to say about my Berkeley experience. At any rate I explained it, pretty much as I have explained it in this chapter; and I also explained why I had no wish to repeat that experience at Washington or anywhere else in the hope that it might turn out better. If all departments really were like Berkeley they were not for me, nor was I at all suitable for them. But I went on to conclude that I still couldn't believe they were; that if he and his department could permit me to teach and do research in my own way, or, more specifically, the way I had been teaching and writing before Berkeley, they might very well find me quite acceptable.

A strange way for anyone to ask for a teaching job. Yet Heilman took it in stride. From first to last he was intelligently if somewhat critically sympathetic, and when I was leaving, and jokingly remarked that I hoped our not being able to agree on a single thing we talked about wouldn't be held against me, he replied, in the same vein, that it wouldn't. Even at the time I think I knew that, all joking aside, it really wouldn't. And when my informal talk with other members of the department, over coffee, turned out to be not only friendly but warm and encouraging, my hopes began to soar. Once again I felt sure that I had lucked out, and once again I was right. In a very few days, on June 29, I received the formal offer of an assistant-professorship.

4

Going My Own Way—
With Departmental Approval
(1948-1951)

W HEN I arrived in Seattle, in the late summer of 1948, the
English department had just been devastated by the Canwell
hearings, which took place in July, and by the succeeding
charges which the president of the University and the board of
regents were bringing against tenured faculty. Of the six finally
charged with present or past membership in the Communist
party three were from English—with several other members of
the department more or less directly involved, including one
professor, an admitted party member in earlier years, who had
felt duty-bound to inform on his fellows. Consequently the
entire English department was thrown into a state of turmoil
that did not really begin to abate until January, 1949, after the
hearings of the Faculty Committee on Tenure and Academic
Freedom and President Allen's recommendations on dismissal
and probation—recommendations which resulted in dismissal
for one member of the English department, probation for two
others.

While it was a dreadful time for me, or anyone else new, to
appear on the scene, it did give me a chance to see how courag-

eously the various members of the department held to their liberal convictions through all the pressures they were having to withstand. And their liberalism seemed to extend to all phases of teaching and academic life: I felt no obligation to lunch at the faculty club (Heilman had already assured me there wouldn't be); no obligation to speak a Seattle version of Lehmanese; no obligation to shun the undergraduates; no obligation to conform to highly structured patterns in either teaching or scholarship. As for the men and women themselves, they seemed, on the positive side, as warm and encouraging as the people I had known and admired at Miami and Cornell and Harvard. The Canwell mentality, given academic sanction in President Allen's policies and designated "the Allen formula," may have prevailed throughout much of the University. But not in the English department. There I felt as free as if I were back at Harvard.

A bit later, after the initial shock of the probations and dismissals had passed, the united front that the department had been maintaining tended to break down—as the philosophical differences between various professors began to split the department into opposing factions, which were loosely but not always accurately labelled Old Parringtonians and New Critics. For Heilman, as well as for the other senior members of the department, the years from 1949 through the early fifties, were years of endless strife and compromise. Heilman, I know, constantly deplored what he called the anarchistic state of the department, even as he himself, greatly to his credit, contributed to that state by his willingness to offer a position to anyone, regardless of his political or critical allegiances or even his academic degrees, who showed promise of doing something really interesting in his teaching or writing. A case in point was the hiring of my good friend George Woodcock, an internationally known anarchist, when no other major university would have given him a second look. And there were numerous others, not so well known, who might not have been acceptable elsewhere but who certainly contributed to the intellectual vigor of the department.

ii

For me, it was the perfect place to be—a department in which there was so much freedom, as well as so much difference and so much conflict, that I could go my own way without getting anyone seriously upset. And everything else in my situation worked out perfectly too. The classes were small, the students responsive, and the actual teaching proved especially exciting because I had numerous courses in the novel which enabled me to apply the new approaches to fiction that I had carried over from Berkeley. During my second year there I had become seriously interested in Freud and psychoanalysis, in relation to literature, and had been fortunate enough to attend the discussions of a small group of analysts in San Francisco who were concerned with the relationship between art and psychoanalysis. Then, at about the same time, I had become acquainted with Stephen Pepper, a professor in the Berkeley philosophy department who invited me, during my final semester at Berkeley, to sit in on his course in aesthetics, where I became acquainted with his version of contextualism, the aesthetic that I would later use, together with Dewey's *Art as Experience*, as the basis for my own theory of fiction.

At the time, however, my attempts to introduce Freud and contextualism into the classroom were at best experimental—as were my attempts to introduce the many other new impressions and influences that came crowding in on me. First there was Celine's *Death on the Installment Plan*, which, along with his *Journey to the End of the Night*, radically altered not only my sense of literature but my sense of life, and sent me, in the summer of 1951, on a pilgrimage to France and Denmark in a vain effort to meet the man himself. What I would have said to Celine, if I had been able to find him, I don't really know. Mainly, I think, I wanted to tell him that he was the greatest novelist in the world; that his novels had done for me what no other novels, or books of any kind, had been able to do—give me a sense of life that could withstand all the efforts of all the idealizers and all the rationalizers in the world who were trying to deny it.

At long last, thanks to Celine's novels, I could see with crystal clarity what I had seen only dimly before: that all the people who had been trying to whip me into shape or make me toe the line were not at all what I had at times thought them to be. They were not villainous, or even mean. They were good citizens bent on driving me into one or another of the self-denying, and therefore life-denying, codes of behavior that they themselves believed in and were trying to impose on themselves. I could see too that my own case was, in many respects, much like that of Celine's hero, Ferdinand (and therefore much like that of Celine himself), the big difference being that I had been incredibly lucky in having a mother and loved ones who had very little sense of good citizenship (no religion, no strong morality, no civic pride) and who were very careful not to impose what sense they did have upon me. For them, in every circumstance, my desires, my feelings came first; everything else second. The saying of a few years back that caused so much amusement, "What's good for General Motors is good for the country," they might, in all honesty and naivete, have modified to read: "What's good for Wayne Burns is good for the world." And that, I could see from Celine's novels, was what had so far saved me from the kind of torment Celine's Ferdinand had suffered at the hands of everyone who tried to reshape him—from his mother and father who loved him to his mixed-up patients (after he became a doctor) who were trying to kill him.

In my unqualified acceptance of Celine's novels I was not only denying Trotsky (who had, for all his understanding and appreciation of Celine's *Journey to the End of the Night*, rejected it on ideological grounds) but also making a final break with the Marxist thinkers and critics whom I had been trying to follow for so many years. By this time I simply had to recognize that my Communist mentor at Duke had been entirely right about my proclivities: that despite my socialist upbringing I could never become a Communist, or a Trotskyite, or a socialist, or even a liberal Democrat; that if I was to become anything that could be given a label I would have to become, as my mentor had predicted, some kind of anarchist. Which was, I suppose, what Mark Schorer meant when, speaking in academic terms, he said I was born to be a Bennington professor; what Douglas Bush meant when he said I would be a viper in the bosom of any English department; what Lehman meant when he said, repeating the very words my scoutmaster and school principal had used so long ago, that I refused to become a member of the team. Seemingly, paraphrasing Schorer, I was born to be an anarchist; and now that I had read Celine I knew the kind of anarchist I wanted to become.

But I also knew, on the basis of the reading I had already done, that I would not find this kind of anarchism in the writings of Godwin, or Proudhon, or Bakunin, or Kropotkin. Much as I responded to their basic libertarian beliefs I invariably had difficulty when they set about developing their own social creeds, which struck me as being either naive or tending towards the very authoritarianism they were seeking to overcome. For that matter I didn't really want a creed; I wanted understanding. More specifically I wanted a philosophical anarchism fully cognizant of Celine's revelations as well as those of Kafka and Camus and other modern writers; an anarchism rooted in Darwin and Freud as well as earlier anarchist thinkers. And I found what I was looking for, after a bit of searching, in the anarchist-pacifist writings of Herbert Read and Alex Comfort and the English New Romantics. The main argument of Comfort's *Art and Social Responsibility* (1946) for example, was that "the war is not between classes. The war is . . . between individuals and barbarian society . . . [which] is rooted today in obedience, conformity, conscription, and the stage has been reached at which, in order to live, you have to be an enemy of society . . . The choice is not between socialism and fascism but between life and obedience." (pp. 38, 83) And in his *The Novel and Our Time* (1948) Comfort went on to show how, in a "totally fragmented society . . ." the serious novel "directs itself to the individual, ignoring all his social connections and ties," finally to bring him to the point where "he sees everyone naked and is as naked himself." (pp. 11, 13, 26)

Then, at just the time when I was absorbing the impact of Read and Comfort, William Carlos Williams came to Washington to give a series of lectures (published in book form as *A Beginning on the Short Story*, 1950) in which he reiterated, even more dramatically, the connections and conflicts that Comfort had stressed. "The finest short stories," Williams declared, "are those that raise, in short, one particular man or woman, from that Gehenna, the newspaper, where at last all men are equal, to the distinction of being an individual. To be responsive not to the ordinances of the herd (Russia like) but to the extraordinary responsibility of being a person. . . . As we write for the magazines today so they [the Russians] write, officially for the Politbureau. But the real writing, the real short story will be written privately, in secret, despairingly—for the individual. For it will be the individual." More poignantly, speaking of the people he was writing about in his own short stories, he went on to explain, "I saw how they were maligned by their institutions of church and state—and 'betters.' I saw how all that was acceptable to the ear maligned them. I saw how stereotype falsified them. . . . It was my duty to raise the level of consciousness, not to say discussion, of them to a higher level, a higher plane. Really to tell." (pp. 7, 8, 11)

These brief excerpts, eloquent as I still find them, hardly give an adequate sense of the lectures themselves, which as I heard them seemed to be not so much lectures as prose poems in which Williams was giving the final word on all matters relating to fiction and society and the individual who was also the artist. That, I know, is how the lectures struck me at the time, although now, as they appear in cold print, much of what Williams is saying, true and eloquent as his words may be, no longer seems all that original or striking. Perhaps when I heard the lectures I was under the spell of Williams' personality: he gave the lectures, as I recall, in a fairly small room to an audience of not more than one hundred and fifty, and in the days following the lectures I had a number of talks with him. Or perhaps it was the way in which his observations and arguments tended to coincide with and validate those of Read and Comfort and the New Romantics. In any event his lectures, coupled with Comfort's books and my other critical reading, stirred me up to such a point that I felt obliged to put together my own version of the relationships between fiction and society and the individual in a lengthy essay entitled "The Novelist as Revolutionary," which appeared in *Arizona Quarterly* (Spring, 1951).

iii

"The Novelist as Revolutionary" brought me quite a few letters, pro and con, when it first appeared, including, on the pro side a note from Philip Rahv in which he suggested that *Partisan Review* might be interested in printing any other essays that I might have lying around if they were of the same quality. Much flattered, I responded by saying that I didn't have anything ready but that I would very much like to write a critical essay on Celine's *Death on the Installment Plan*, if *Partisan* was interested, since I considered it one of the great novels of our time that had never received the critical attention it deserved. I also mentioned that I was writing an essay on Alex Comfort's novels that I expected to complete soon. Then, in what must have been the return mail, I received a reply in which Rahv, assuming I was naive, which in one sense of course I was, proceeded to inform me that Celine was one of the world's most dangerous anti-Semites, and that so long as he, Philip Rahv, had anything to do with *Partisan* no favorable criticism of Celine's work would ever appear in its pages. To which he added by way of postscript: Comfort is simply not in the mainstream of things. Why don't you do something on Graham Greene. Even when I first received this letter I could, in part at least, recognize Rahv's good intentions, right down to his crassly commercial dismissal of Comfort, but that didn't prevent me from being terribly disillusioned—to the point of feeling that still another bastion of intellectual freedom, one that I had over the years looked upon as more free and open than even the most liberal English department, had surrendered its position, that Rahv was more closely related to Paull Baum than I had ever dreamed possible.

"The Novelist as Revolutionary" also involved me in much discussion with my colleagues at Washington, and if I were trying to give a full account of my critical activities, I would feel obliged to discuss the nature and merits of the essay at some length. But my primary concern here is not with my criticism, as criticism, but with what the criticism reveals about my teaching; and for that purpose, it seems to me, I need to indicate only my primary argument in the essay, which was, as I expressed it in the essay itself, to show why the serious novelist has no choice but to be "irresponsible," or, as Comfort had put it, to be at war with society and its institutions:

> The novelist, like the scientist, must be free to follow his "madness" (what I prefer to call his "difference") wherever it leads . . . For his ultimate function is to express his own particular "difference," or as it is more commonly designated, his own genius, his own vision of reality. It follows, therefore, that if the novelist would be true to his artistic function, he must perforce be a revolutionary—in the sense that every creative scientist is a revolutionary. He must discover and define what he conceives to be the new realities; and to do this, he must try to push beyond the existing frontiers of knowledge and experience. At this stage of the creative process he is already struggling towards revolution; and if he succeeds in his artistic quest, if he uses form in such a way as to make us realize that his difference, his reality, is a true and significant one, then he has become the ultimate artist— and incidentally the ultimate revolutionary. This is the way, thus far the only way, that the creative imagination can find expression in fiction. . . . It may not be easy to grant the novelist so much, especially when his intention seems immoral, unpatriotic, irreligious, or generally subversive of established values. Yet for better or worse those are the only terms he can accept, and still remain true to his function. This is the price of

modern fictional art; and if we are to pay that price, we must be prepared to accept and encourage the serious novelist as we do the scientist—as a kind of licensed madman and revolutionary.

Of the many ways in which my arguments in this essay carried over to my teaching perhaps the most basic was the way that I had, by implication, begun to extend my argument concerning the novelist and the scientist to include me as professor of literature. Not that I saw myself or any other professor as creative in the sense that the novelist and scientist were. My function, like that of any like-minded English professor, was, as I conceived of it, the more modest one of re-creation. Just as the novelist followed his difference wherever it might lead, so the literature professor, together with his class, followed the novelist, in his difference, wherever his novel might lead, ultimately to bring the novel to what R. P. Blackmur called "full artistic performance."

So stated my view of the professorial function in literature would have seemed quite acceptable to just about everyone, including New Critics. Where I became radically deviant was in my conception of the novelist as necessarily "irresponsible" and at war with society—a conception which clearly implied that the English professor who taught the novels would necessarily have to be "irresponsible" too, in the same way and to the same degree as the novelist. True, he would, in a sense, be "irresponsible" at second hand: he would stand in relation to the novel he was teaching in much the same way writers in the past had stood in relation to their muse. But he would still, for all practical purposes, have to take his stand with the novel, against society and its institutions and its values.

What made this view seem Quixotic—even to my otherwise sympathetic friends and colleagues—was my insistence on the word "necessarily." Some few novels might be "irresponsible" and at war with society, they argued, but most were not, and there was consequently no need for me to get myself, and anyone else who would listen, all stirred up with irresponsible talk about all professors having to become irresponsible. The professor's responsibility, as they saw it, was rather to present a more objective reading of the novels—a reading which would show that they were not at war with society at all; or that if they were, they were not at war with society as such, only with society's bad aspects or values or institutions. If I continued to find all serious novels "irresponsible," they argued further, it would be because I was setting out with the presupposition that they were, and then reading in what I hoped to find.

These arguments I countered by pointing out that the charge of "reading in" was double-edged; that, besides, there is such a thing as reading out. Why, if I was hoping to find serious novels "irresponsible," wasn't it just as likely that they, under the guise of objectivity, were hoping to find them "responsible," in line with their own presuppositions? But there was nothing to be gained, I recognized, by such charges and countercharges. The real test, I readily conceded, was what the works themselves revealed, through close textual analysis. Yet even that test, I well knew, had its limitations, since what the works themselves would reveal through close analysis would in large measure be determined by the presuppositions of the person doing the analysis. If I, for example, drawing upon the increased understanding of human motivations I had gained through Freud, found sexual implications in a novel that were simply not there for another reader, how could I prove to him that they were there?

iv

For the time being I had no answers to these critical questions that would satisfy either me or my colleagues. But I was working some out in my classes, where, in different ways, I confronted the same critical questions day after day—most directly perhaps in a course entitled "Introduction to Fiction," in which we had as one of our primary texts Brooks and Warren's *Understanding Fiction*, the one textbook that overlooked or denied or contradicted everything I felt or perceived or believed in.

The distance that separated me from Brooks and Warren

can hardly be measured: whereas they believed in and constantly invoked "good" and "evil" in their commentaries these words
had little if any meaning for me. Of course I knew what they
were supposed to mean. As a student I had even had a go at trying to endow them with emotional meaning in reading Milton
and other Christian writers. But the notion that "evil" could, in
the middle of the twentieth century, be invoked outside of, or
apart from, a specific religious faith, struck me as being a
dangerously reactionary attempt to impose a religious morality
in the guise of objective commentary, a morality which Brooks
and Warren developed much further through their invocation
of "code," "obedience," "sin," "fidelity," "discipline," "ideal,"
"order," and yes, even "honor"—words and concepts that I
found either quaint or anathema. Nor could I even begin to
accept their formalist criticism itself, premised on their belief, as
Brooks stated it in another connection, "that the primary
concern of criticism is with the problem of unity—the kind of
whole which the literary work forms or fails to form, and the
relation of the various parts to each other in building up this
whole." To me—and I am not now trying to denigrate their
theory of criticism, only to state my reaction to it—their formalist approach denied vision, meaning, in a word, art, and
would, if consistently applied, turn fictional works into high-
level technical puzzles.

Actually Brooks and Warren did not, in their commentaries
in *Understanding Fiction*, adhere closely to their own formalist
principles. But what they did do was perhaps worse. Again and
again, in the guise of objective critics, they trundled in their
Christian-traditional-moral machinery, with which they then
ran over every single story in the book—all the while justifying
the process in terms of unity, structure, symbolism and irony.
And what was most upsetting to me at the time: they not only
did all this with consummate skill, they did it in complete good
faith. They weren't academic hucksters, trying to sell books;
they were men who believed in what they were trying to do—
which, as they conceived of it, was nothing less than the introduction of a new and vital form of criticism into the academy.

So that, however absurd and misguided and deadly I found

their criticism I felt that I had to take it seriously. As a practical matter, in the course itself, I had no choice. Their commentaries were right there, immediately following the stories, in the same format, the same print, as the stories themselves. Indeed I wondered at times if some of the students were fully aware of where the stories left off and the "interpretations" began. In some instances too, the interpretations came close to being as long and detailed as the stories themselves—as if Brooks and Warren were afraid that some student might find some detail that might lead him astray.

A case in point is their "interpretation" of Sherwood Anderson's "I Want to Know Why," in which they begin by pointing out that, "This story, like 'The Killers,' by Hemingway, is a story of the 'initiation.' That is, the hero—a boy, as in 'The Killers'—discovers something about the nature of evil." Then they go on for some six pages (the story itself is eight pages long) explaining why the boy, who loves race horses to the point of obsession, gets terribly upset when he sees a horse trainer whom he admires looking at a prostitute with the same "shine in his eyes" that he had earlier bestowed on the boy himself. Brooks and Warren's six pages of explanation are, as might be expected, much preoccupied with questions of "evil" (e.g., "The horse (nature) is not capable of evil or of goodness, which depend upon human choice")—questions which they finally resolve in a concluding paragraph:

> In the beginning of this analysis it was said that this story is, like Hemingway's "The Killers," the story of an "initiation." Not that evil exists, for he had known for a long time that there are good and bad people—that is, he was acquainted with the ordinary conventional definitions. But he discovers that good and bad are very intimately wedded in the very nature of a man, and, perhaps more importantly still, that it is man's capacity for choice which makes good and evil meaningful.

Then, as if vaguely aware that they have turned the story into a moral platitude, they add still another concluding paragraph in which they argue that a platitude is not a platitude when it is presented dramatically, in terms of experience:

> Having said this, having extracted what may seem to be a moral "message," one should remind himself that the "message" is, as such, not the story. The story may be said to be the dramatization of the discovery. Now the message is something of which everyone is aware; it is a platitude. But the platitude ceases to be a platitude, it is revitalized and becomes meaningful again, when it is shown to be operating in terms of experience. (p. 349)

Brooks and Warren's argument would have given me fits—even if they had been right about the story. But they weren't. The platitude that so worried them and that they were so bent upon revitalizing was of their own making, and had little if anything to do with the story, which was not about a boy's discovery of "something about the nature of evil," but rather about a boy's discovery of something about the nature of sex. Or, more accurately, it is about the reader's discovery, through the boy, since the boy cannot understand why he feels the way he does about the man and about horses; why, when he sees the man kiss the prostitute, he begins "to hate that man," and wants "to scream and rush in the room and kill him." But the story makes certain that the reader understands, provided he is willing and able to give the words of the story their direct meaning and implications; and what the reader understands, put in the most crude general terms, is that the boy's adolescent passion for the man is a homosexual passion—a passion which he will in all probability outgrow, but which, at this time, so overwhelms him that he cannot witness the man's kissing a woman (the fact that the woman is a prostitute is, for the boy, a moral screen) without wanting "to kill him." Or, as the boy himself puts it, in the last two lines of the story: "Sometimes I'm so mad about it I want to fight someone. It gives me the fantods. What did he do it for? I want to know why."

Such was my reading of the story, and I was firmly con-

vinced that it made nonsense out of Brooks and Warren's elaborate interpretation. But my aim here is not to defend my reading, or attack theirs; my aim is rather to suggest what a dilemma
I was confronted with in teaching *Understanding Fiction*. For my
readings of the other stories in the book also tended to contradict Brooks and Warren's interpretations at every turn.

Unless I was going to surrender my own position, my own
critical perceptions, I therefore had to fight it out with Brooks
and Warren in the classroom—and seemingly they had all the
advantages. They were authors, and therefore authorities; they
reached the students first; their beliefs and values would have
more appeal for the students than my own; their interpretations
would be more in line with what the students had come to expect in English classes. In the actual classroom, however, these
advantages did not prove overwhelming. The students were impressed with Brooks and Warren, to be sure, but not to the
point that they couldn't understand my objections to the entire
New Critical approach. And when I went on to encourage them,
first to question Brooks and Warren's interpretations, then,
with my help, to work out alternative interpretations of their
own, their responses far exceeded my expectations. In discussing
"I Want to Know Why," for instance, they arrived at an interpretation essentially like the one I have presented here; and
they did this on their own, with a minimum of prompting from
me.

v

I have stressed my classroom battle with Brooks and Warren
because it marked a new departure for me. Up to this point I
had never, in teaching my classes, been obliged to define my
own critical position in such forthright terms. Yet if I was going
to fight Brooks and Warren's "evil" I simply had to. Otherwise
the students would never have understood either my objections
or my position. And I discovered, once I had been forced into
definition, that everything else seemed to go better—presum-

ably because, with a clear notion of where I was coming from, critically and philosophically, the students could more readily accept my specific observations and interpretations, which no longer seemed quite so outrageous or so radical. They could see, for example, that I wasn't trying to shock them or titillate them with the sexuality in "I Want to Know Why," that my reading of the story, which many of them arrived at on their own, was every bit as intelligent and perceptive in my terms as Brooks and Warren's was in theirs.

There were other salutary effects too. More tenuous, to be sure, but nevertheless genuine. For if I could quarrel with Brooks and Warren, the students could too. More than that, they could also quarrel with me, and not be too upset if I quarreled with them. They were learning how to question authority, including my authority, and in the process they were learning the rudiments of intellectual discussion—primarily the ability to entertain different ideas, different points of view, without turning them into personal contests or personal attacks. They were learning that they could say anything to me or anyone else in class, so long as they were reasonably polite, without fear of ridicule or reprisal of any kind. They were, in short, learning that they could trust me.

Needless to say I didn't realize all these advantages at one fell swoop, in a single class, as a result of my classroom battle with Brooks and Warren. But the extent to which I did realize them showed me that the battle, and the stand I was obliged to take in order to fight it, provided me with just the dramatic format I needed in the classroom—a format that I could use in practically all of my courses. *Understanding Fiction* wouldn't be there, but there were New Critics everywhere—the New Criticism, as I have indicated, had begun to sweep the country—and I could, without too much difficulty, assign outside reading in articles or books that would provide me with exactly the type of conflict that I was looking for. Indeed, by re-defining and extending the conflict to include all the major schools of criticism, I could use the same basic format in graduate courses and seminars.

Whether or not these possibilities were as clear in my mind as I have suggested I am no longer certain. But I do know that I immediately set about redesigning my courses along the lines I have indicated, and with excellent results, especially in the senior-graduate courses in the English novel that I was teaching, where my new format gave me a better chance to win the confidence of the students and thus establish the bond of trust that I have spoken of. At this level, as well as in the straight graduate courses, the bond became much more difficult to establish than in the introductory courses: the students were not only older and more sophisticated; they were also, not to mince words, far more distrustful of their professors. Yet for the kind of teaching I was trying to do they had to trust me. For I was constantly asking them, in class, to deal with aspects of the novels, primarily aspects of character, that impinged directly upon their own conception of themselves and their fellows and the world they lived in, oftentimes in terms that were new and strange to them.

If it seems that what I am saying here tends to repeat what I said earlier, I must acknowledge that it does. But there are differences. The demands I made on students in my earlier classes at Miami, and Cornell, and Harvard and Berkeley were essentially of the same kind, and in terms of the varying situations perhaps equally great. But for the most part I was then teaching introductory classes, and limiting my demands to what I believed were the students' capabilities. The exceptions were my classes at Harvard and Radcliffe and a few of my classes at Berkeley, in which, for the reasons I have already suggested, the students seemed more trusting, more willing to confront the implications of serious fiction. Yet what happened in those classes (that is, where we went and how we got there) was more the result of the students' perceptiveness and enthusiasm than anything I myself contributed. All of which was great, of course, in those particular classes. At that time the best I could do was offer a few critical suggestions, plus a few of my own reactions, and hope they would get the students going.

By the time I got to Washington, however, I had a better sense of what I could contribute. Thanks to Freud and Celine and all the other reading I had been doing, I understood more; and thanks to my teaching experiences I had a better sense of how I could put my new understanding to work in the classroom—without trying to overwhelm the students with it. This last point was crucial. No matter how great my own understanding I could never, in the kind of teaching I was trying to do, impose it on the students. They had to be free to go where they would. But I could stir them up in the ways that I thought might lead to the most interesting explorations of the works we were reading; and as I gained a fuller sense of my function, and began to realize the advantages that the dramatic format I had derived from my conflict with Brooks and Warren offered me, I ventured further and further into the connections between art and experience—in an effort to get the students to make their own connections.

In discussing *Jane Eyre*, for example, there was no escaping the sexuality that permeates every aspect of the novel, from Jane's experience in the red room to the final scene in which she dallies with the physical hulk of her shorn Samson. Nor was there any escaping—and this is where the discussion became really difficult for many students—the connection between Jane's sexuality and her Methodism. At one point in the discussion, in an effort to clarify the connection, I tried reading an extended passage from the novel aloud in class (the passage in which St. John is once again pressing Jane to marry him, this time for the greater glory of God) omitting much of the commentary as well as some of the dramatic lines, as in the following excerpts, but with no hints as to what I had found in the passage:

> He laid his hand on my head as he uttered the last words. . . . All men of talent, whether they be men of feeling or not; whether they be zealots, or aspirants, or despots—provided only they be sincere—have their sublime moments: when they subdue and rule. I felt veneration for St. John—veneration so strong that its impetus thrust me at once to the point I had so long shunned. I was tempted to cease struggling with him—to rush

down the torrent of his will into the gulf of his existence, and there lose my own. I was almost as hard beset by him now as I had been once before, in a different way, by another. . . .

I stood motionless under my hierophant's touch. My refusals were forgotten—my fears overcome—my wrestlings paralysed. The Impossible—*i.e.* my marriage with St. John—was fast becoming the Possible. All was changing utterly, with a sudden sweep. Religion called—Angels beckoned—God commanded—life rolled together like a scroll—death's gates opening, showed eternity beyond: it seemed, that for safety and bliss there, all here might be sacrificed in a second. The dim room was full of visions.

"Could you decide now?"asked the missionary. The inquiry was put in gentle tones: he drew me to him gently. Oh, that gentleness! how far more potent is it than force! I could resist St. John's wrath: I grew pliant as a reed under his kindness. . . .

"My prayers are heard!" ejaculated St. John. He pressed his hand firmer on my head, as if he claimed me: he surrounded me with his arm, almost as if he loved me. (I say almost—I knew the difference—for I had felt what it was to be loved; but, like him, I had now put love out of the question, and thought only of duty): I contended with my inward dimness of vision, before which clouds yet rolled. I sincerely, deeply, fervently longed to do what was right; and only that. "Show me, show me the path!" I entreated of Heaven.

I was excited more than I had ever been. . . .

My heart beat fast and thick: I heard its throb. Suddenly it stood still to an inexpressible feeling that thrilled it through, and passed at once to my head and extremities. The feeling was not like an electric shock; but it was quite as sharp, as strange, as startling: it acted on my senses as if their utmost activity hitherto had been but torpor, from which they were now summoned, and forced to wake. They rose expectant: eye and ear waited, while the flesh quivered on my bones. . . .

"I am coming!" I cried. "Wait for me! Oh I will come!" . . .

I recalled that inward sensation I had experienced: for I could recall it, with all its unspeakable strangeness. . . . The wondrous shock of feeling had come like the earthquake which shook the foundations of Paul and Silas's prison. . .

Although I included much more of the text than I have reproduced here, I tried to keep my entire reading objective, even flat. Then, without any further preliminaries, I asked what was going on in the passage, what was Jane experiencing. The question, I could see, made for considerable uneasiness until someone in the class—I don't remember just who—said rather tentatively: "She's having an orgasm." Sometimes, when a student comes out with something that no one else has seen or thought of, his words will bring a collective gasp from the rest of the students—as they absorb the shock. But in this instance there was no gasp. It was as if the student's words expressed the other students' own perceptions, their own understanding—almost to a man or woman. The "almost" is necessary because, in the discussion which followed, everyone seemed to be in general agreement until one member of the class, a woman in her early twenties, burst into a fit of uncontrolled sobbing and had to be led from the classroom by a fellow student. What happened, although I had no way of knowing this at the time, was that the woman had, through my reading of the passage and the discussion which followed, come to the sudden realization that her own religious experiences—experiences which she had always believed to be spiritual epiphanies—had in fact been orgasmic as well.

For the woman herself, I am happy to report, the shock of recognition, painful as it was at the time, did not seem to have any lasting ill effects. In fact she later came to see the effects as beneficial. Yet I still felt uneasy, not only about this particular episode but about others of a similar nature which had begun occurring with more and more frequency—episodes which seemed to indicate that what we were doing in class might, if one or more students were seriously mixed up to start with, have really dangerous consequences. And while I tried to convince myself, as I had done earlier at Harvard and Berkeley, that the risk was not all that great, and that anyway I had no choice, I never could overcome my apprehensions. I simply had to live with them as best I could.

The one thing I could never do, of course, no matter how apprehensive I became, was to permit my apprehensions to dictate the terms of class discussion. The day after the young woman I have been speaking of broke into her fit of weeping, for example, I reopened the discussion of the passage in *Jane Eyre* just as if nothing untoward had happened. And the class responded beautifully, not only confirming everything that had been said the day before but going much further—to bring out implications in the passage that had never before appeared in print, and that would provide me with the basis for a reinterpretation of *Jane Eyre* in *Literature and Psychology*.

vi

The graduate seminar on Dickens that I gave my second year at Washington also worked out extremely well. My first aim in the seminar, a negative one, was to get away from the traditional format which was still being used by many professors, even at Washington—a format in which the professor indicated the type of subject, or perhaps even the specific subject, that each student was to work up into a paper; then himself sat back and listened while the students droned on, taking turns giving papers that bored everyone, including the professor, whose only real interest, as often as not, lay in the possibility that some bright graduate student might come up with evidence or ideas that he might incorporate, with or without due acknowledgment, in a book he was working on.

After sitting through bromidic seminars of this type as a graduate student I could hardly bring myself to assume the professorial role in one of my own. What I had in mind was a type which would do just what I had been doing in my undergraduate classes—only do it more intensely, more inclusively, and more self-consciously. To that end I retained my dramatic format, defined my own critical position, including, of course, its Freudian components; and then, by way of giving the students a new perspective on Dickens, one that would oblige them to connect Dickens' novels up with their own experience in as yet untried ways, I asked them to read, first Kafka's *Amerika*, then Celine's *Death on the Installment Plan*. The effect of Kafka's novel I could anticipate fairly well, since I had used it earlier in a seminar at Berkeley. It was *Death on the Installment Plan* which had me worried. And with good reason. For the novel provoked responses as powerful as they were radically diverse, some students declaring it the greatest novel they had ever read, others, equally vehement, finding nothing in it but filth. I can, for instance, recall one student's remarking that he didn't see why he should bother making connections with Celine's novel, since he could get the same effect by sticking his head in the toilet bowl. Whereupon another student, replying in kind, observed that the first student seemed better acquainted with the toilet bowl than with the novel. For a time, indeed, it looked as if the seminar might degenerate into a series of shouting matches. But the students' tempers, as well as their manners, improved considerably once I got them past Celine's novel, and it soon became apparent that the verbal battles they had gone through had left them in just the kind of aroused state I had been hoping to get them into. For I soon had otherwise sedate or blase graduate students embroiled in heated discussions about everything from the ways in which Celine's and Kafka's heroes resembled Dickens' to the ways in which the worlds these novelists created connected up with the real world in which they themselves lived.

At times these discussions generated far more heat than light; at other times, however, the light shone through—as the discussions led me as well as the students into as yet unexplored areas of Dickens' world, areas that we would never have known were there if we had not approached the novels the way we did. Nor did these explorations end when the classes ended. A few of the students carried them much further in their seminar papers, which even now, as I look through them some thirty years later, still seem remarkably perceptive.

But I don't mean to suggest that sweetness and light eventually prevailed in the seminar. For some students it never appeared at all. One man, an older graduate student from the history department who found my Freudian emphases intolerable, regularly went into gyrations to express his hatred of just about everything that I said, leaning over behind the student next to him, where, I suppose, he thought I couldn't see him, and shaking his fist in rage. It was a truly Dickensian performance, but it was also, as he later explained, seriously intended: he was trying to express his sense of outrage at the way, in his words, I and the other people in the seminar were turning Dickens' novels into twentieth-century snake pits of our own construction.

With the man's particular viewpoint—he wanted to return to the old sentimental, Christmassy Dickens—I didn't have much sympathy. Nevertheless his words did give me pause for other reasons, since I could see that his charges were at least partially true, that some students were exploiting my suggestions, and more particularly my Freudian suggestions, in ways I never intended. What worried me the most was their tendency, perhaps the result of their greater literary sophistication, combined as it was for many of them with undergraduate training in New Criticism, to turn my talk about connections into a license for hunting them—the way so many New Critics hunted symbols. One graduate student, for instance, gave a quite ingenious paper in which he insisted, at length and in detail, on a Freudian interpretation of all the keys in all the locks in *Martin Chuzzlewit*—an interpretation that parodied, though quite unintentionally, everything I had been trying to do in the seminar. It wasn't just that I had been misunderstood, that one of the brightest students in the class had written a silly paper, and that many people in the class seemed incapable of recognizing its silliness. What really upset me was something even more basic—their inability to recognize the difference between experiencing a novel and doing ingenious exercises upon it.

vii

Yet my disappointments in the seminar, and in my other classes as well, were far outweighed by what I felt were my very real achievements. If I had not quite become the teacher I wanted to be, the teacher I envisioned in my "Novelist as Revolutionary," I was nevertheless getting there. More amazing still, I was getting there with the help and seemingly the approval of nearly everyone in the English department, New Critics and Old Parringtonians alike. Some of the goings-on in my classes had become, as might be expected, the talk of Parrington Hall (the building in which the English department had its offices and classes). Yet the talk never became really vicious, as gossip so often does. Or if it did I never had to feel the brunt of it. At the height of the furor Celine's novel created in my Dickens seminar, when the TA's in the class were giving verbatim reports on the insults they were hurling at each other, a few of my colleagues did, understandably, express concern. But it was all very friendly—as in one man's good natured query as to whether or not I was planning to call in the campus police.

Heilman too was fully aware of what I was doing in my classes. Indeed he may have been more aware than anyone else, since I taught the same sequence of courses in the English novel that he did (a quarter behind him) and he was constantly being reminded by students of the great differences between his courses and mine. And while the comparisons, I'm certain, were no more in my favor than his, he may still have found them a bit hard to take, if only because he would have preferred to have the courses listed in the catalogue under the same numbers bear some resemblance to each other. But if he was disappointed in my teaching he never once said so. Nor did he use any of the roundabout tactics for expressing disapproval that I had become accustomed to at Berkeley. I continued to talk with him about many things, and we continued to disagree about most of them, but with mutual respect, and, on my side, sincere admiration for his willingness, as chairman, to put up with my dissident views.

Yet, happy as I was to have the approval of the department at Washington, it never ceased to amaze me, and, on another level, puzzle and worry me. Not the approval itself. I had, as I have indicated, enjoyed departmental approval as a teacher at

Miami and Cornell and Harvard, and in each instance I had been able to accept it pretty much as a matter of course without really thinking very much about it. But the terms in which it had been granted in those instances were different. At Miami I was a former student, returning as a teacher, presumably for a period of apprenticeship; at Cornell the conditions had been much the same; and at Harvard, although I became a full-fledged member of the department, English A wasn't, in the usual academic sense, a department at all but rather—and this is what I found so great about it—a loosely knit group of people teaching English together for a period of, at most, five years or so. In all of these instances, therefore, I could accept the approval, and even be grateful for it, without feeling that my acceptance bound me to anything.

At Berkeley, however, the situation had been different. There, as in any department offering a position that might eventually become tenured, approval could only be granted on the assumption, spoken or unspoken, that the person accepting the position had committed himself to the values or attitudes of the department granting it. Of course the person could lie or pretend, if he chose, in order to secure tenure or promotion, but in that case he would be breaking faith with those who had granted the approval. Much of this I think I understood, in theory at least, before I went to Berkeley. What I didn't understand, of course, even after my experience with Paull Baum at Duke, was the extent to which departmental approval could depend upon prescribed values and attitudes that I couldn't possibly accept. Once I understood that, needless to say, I also understood that I no longer had to worry about approval—just disapproval, which in some ways was easier for me to deal with. Easier because, from childhood on, I had never been a fully committed member of any team, never tried to win the approval of any group or institution. If approval came that was fine; if disapproval I might argue, as I did with Lehman in the beginning, that I really deserved approval. But that was as far as I could go. I couldn't change in an effort to overcome the disapproval and win approval. I simply had to quit teaching altogether or go somewhere else.

In choosing the latter alternative and going to Washington I was of course hoping that the members of the English department there might grant me the approval Berkeley had withheld—not because I had become different or better but because their values and attitudes were so much more open and liberal than Berkeley's. Yet I never expected that the liberalism would extend so far, or that the approval would be so complete and ungrudging for so long a time—by the spring of 1951 three full years. And while I couldn't help feeling pleased, even grateful, I likewise couldn't help wondering why I had never once been seriously challenged in my dissidence. After all some of the things I had been saying and writing simply had to be upsetting to at least some members of the department—unless they were excusing me as a youthful enthusiast who would eventually grow up; or trying to dismiss me as a misguided but harmless Freudian (the label I was often being tagged with at that time); or, and this possibility really worried me, unless they were expecting me to respond to their gestures of approval with conciliatory gestures of my own. For those were gestures that I knew I could never make.

It wasn't that I wanted to be disagreeable. I never did enjoy being different, or difficult, or contradictory, or in any sense at odds with other people. Actually I wanted to be agreeable. I liked people, and I liked the sense of camaraderie I felt when I could be emotionally at one with them—the sense I had, for example, during the first few meetings of almost every class I taught, before I had to introduce concepts that invariably tended to alienate many of the students. Likewise the sense I had in talking with some of my colleagues in the hall, or over coffee, before the talk became serious and, as so often happened, I either had to interject a disturbing observation or refuse to say anything at all, since I had never learned to dissemble, never learned to take refuge in the usual kind of witty academic chit-chat.

So that, however much I wanted to be agreeable, however much I wanted to respond positively to the approval being accorded me, there always came a time when I had to show my colors in all their individualist and anarchist hues. On such occasions I couldn't help wondering if there might come a time when the department could no longer put up with my dissident behavior, when, in short, even a department so amazingly open and liberal as Washington continued to be would have to withdraw its approval. I didn't want to think such thoughts; I just couldn't help myself. Nor could I help thinking that my time as a professor might consequently be short, and that I should therefore make the most of it not only in the classroom, as I had been doing, but also in my scholarly and critical writing.

viii

Why scholarly research continued to fascinate me, even while I was so deeply engrossed in teaching and criticism, I now find difficult to explain. In part, I'm sure, it was a carry-over from my undergraduate days, when, thanks primarily to A. W. Craver, I had developed so much youthful admiration for great works of interpretive scholarship such as John Livingston Lowes' *Road to Xanadu*, to cite only one example, that I could think of nothing more exciting or meaningful than undertaking such a work on my own. And I still felt much the same way when I wrote my dissertation. Not that I saw it as a great book, or even a book. But I thought that I had the makings of a great scholarly book in the manuscripts and incredibly voluminous notebooks of Charles Reade which were available in the London Library, and I made plans to go to England and start work on the book as early as 1945 while I was still finishing up my dissertation at Cornell.

Then, as I became more and more engrossed in my teaching, and in criticism, and as I went through my traumatic years at Berkeley, I kept putting my scholarly plans aside. Although I still believed in them, and still intended to carry them out, I could see how long and arduous the research would be, not to mention the writing itself, which for me, as a slow writer, might take not just months but years. These considerations, given my overwhelming interest in teaching and criticism, were certainly discouraging, as were the well-intentioned words of advice I was beginning to get from my friends, about my needing a book to ensure my tenure. I still couldn't think in such terms, or accept such advice. To me it seemed demeaning. Nor would I have been any better off, practically speaking, if I had been able to accept it, since the book I had in mind was, I knew, years away.

What finally got me started on the book, despite all my reasons for continuing to delay, were personal considerations having little to do with my academic situation. I wanted to get away from home for a while, and, on the positive side, I wanted to go to England and Europe while I still could. McCarthyism, by 1951, had become so much of a threat to anyone with my past Communist affiliations that it seemed as if just getting a passport might be a problem. Certainly I knew that I would never get one if I acknowledged my intention to visit Celine, in France or in a Danish prison, or my intention to talk with Alex Comfort and other anarchist writers and critics in England. Research was my best cover, and since, deep down, I really wanted to get started on the book anyway, that was how I arranged for two quarters leave with the English department and the University.

5

The Teacher as Revolutionary
(1952–1959)

MY TRIP abroad could hardly have gone better. Although I didn't get to see Celine, despite all my efforts, I did manage to do a 1951 version of the grand tour, then settled down in London to work on the Reade manuscripts in the London Library. The work too went very well, if very slowly; and on weekends I met and talked with Alex Comfort and a number of other writers and critics, mostly anarchist, whom I met at an international writers' conference in London—none of them very well known but all extremely knowledgeable in matters relating to the English literary scene.

Because of the people I met at the writers' conference I would have to count it as one of the high points of my stay in London. But it also served to remind me of what I had left behind in the U.S. and would be returning to very soon. The conference included writers from all of Europe, including a number from behind the Iron Curtain—a fact that I was aware of but did not think much about until a young American novelist, whom I had met on the way in to the opening session, first pointed out that the two of us seemed to be the only Americans there, and then went on to observe that we could not afford to be seen associating with so many Communists. By this time we had sat down, and while I was still trying to figure out whether he had been serious in his remarks, he all of a sudden dived from his seat onto the floor, where, lying prone, he pointed to a camera that was being aimed at us (by, as it turned out, a photographer from *The Manchester Guardian*) and refused to get up until the photographer promised to desist. Then, after apologizing for his strange antics, he went on to explain why they were necessary: his wife, who was his sole support, worked in the American embassy in Paris, and if the embassy learned that he had attended a writers' conference with Reds in it, his wife would be fired the next day.

At the time I couldn't believe McCarthyism had got that bad; I thought my new friend must be over-reacting. But it didn't take me long, once I returned to this country, to find out that nearly all my liberal and radical friends were acting much the same way—seemingly with good reason. Nor were they the only ones. I can recall sitting in the office of a colleague soon after my return to Seattle, and being surprised when he took time, after meeting his class, to jot down what seemed to be notes. And when I asked him, jokingly I thought, why he prepared his notes after class rather than before, he informed me, in all seriousness, that he was keeping a record of what he said in class—in case he was called before the Un-American Activities Committee. The class, I should point out, was a class in Renaissance literature, and the professor himself had never been involved in radical activities of any kind. Nevertheless, as he went on to explain, "In these times one can't be too careful."

Once again I couldn't believe that there was any real justification for such actions and words. For that matter I still don't. But at the same time I have to acknowledge that I may have been as foolhardy in one direction as my colleague was careful in the other. For I never thought twice about the risks involved in applying for a Guggenheim Fellowship when, in the fall of 1952, I decided that my stay in England had been far too short, and that I might do well to apply for a Guggenheim to complete my work on the Reade manuscripts. While I did, as I recall, have to state somewhere in my application that I had never been a member of the Communist Party, I could do that without any qualms. Nor did any of the other questions I had to answer so much as give me pause. If I thought about my FBI record and the attorney general's ominous words, and I'm sure I did, I must have presumed that, in the unlikely event they came to light, the Guggenheim people would understand.

In any event I remained sanguine, and in April of 1953 the good news came. The secretary of the Guggenheim Foundation wrote to inform me that I was about to receive a Fellowship, or words to that effect, and that they now needed to have my exact itinerary, along with a few other necessary details concerning my plans, in order to figure out exactly how much money I would receive. It seemed a strange way to do things—to work out all these details before actually granting the Fellowship— but others in the department who had received Fellowships assured me that I had nothing to worry about, that it was all settled. Then, just when I was beginning to believe them, I received a phone call from the secretary of the Foundation in New York, asking me if I could meet him at ten the next morning at the Olympic Hotel. At first, thinking perhaps he was confused as to my whereabouts, I asked him if he knew where I was, and if he actually meant the Olympic Hotel in Seattle. To which he replied, cordially enough, that he knew I was in Seattle; that he was flying out to see me; that I shouldn't worry, but that it really was terribly important.

Even at this point I hadn't the slightest notion as to what the difficulty might be. Although I presumed it must have something to do with my past Communist affiliations, I was hardly prepared for the secretary's telling me, once we were past the usual amenities, that the difficulties had to do with my present affiliations. Had I, he questioned, seen the latest issue of the *American Mercury* (May, 1953) in which I was being cited, in an article by J. B. Matthews entitled "Communism and the Colleges," as one of the most dangerous Communists or Communist-fronters in the U.S.? Needless to say, I hadn't seen the article. In fact I continued to think that there must be some mistake until he showed me the actual page (123) on which my name appeared, along with my crime—nothing less than my having acted as a sponsor, along with one hundred and three other professors, for the Mid-Century Conference for Peace.

If it hadn't been so dreadfully serious it would have been ludicrous, as the secretary could see clearly enough. But he could also see what I had not yet come to see clearly: that the charge itself didn't matter. Ludicrous as it might be, even without my history as a CO, it nevertheless put my name on the McCarthy list, and if I received a Fellowship McCarthy's investigators would track down everything I had ever done, everything I had ever signed, everything I had ever said—from Georgetown up to the present. All this the secretary pointed out before he asked me the question he had come all the way to Seattle to ask: "What will they find?"

It seemed a fair enough question, in the circumstances, and I tried to answer it fairly, giving him a much more detailed account of my radical history than I have given in this book, and offering to provide him with all kinds of documentation in support of what I had been saying. At this point he said, quite graciously, that he didn't need proof; that he believed every word I had said. "More than that," he continued, "I've read every word you've ever written, and I'm not only convinced that you aren't a Communist; I'm convinced you never could have been one." Thinking this was extremely fair, as well as extremely perceptive, I was about to breathe a sigh of relief when he quickly added: "But it doesn't matter." What I had told him, he went on to explain, showed that there was no real basis for a McCarthy attack but it also showed that I would be vulnerable if one were launched—as it almost certainly would be if I were granted a Fellowship. And, he explained further, if I were vulnerable the Guggenheim Foundation would be vulnerable. In the circumstances, he concluded, it was his job to protect both me and the Foundation—a job he could best fulfill, he believed, if he could persuade me to withdraw my application (I couldn't resign it, since I hadn't actually received it yet) for the present, with the understanding that it might be considered favorably at some future time when McCarthyism was no longer such a threat.

I liked the secretary; I even believed that he would try to keep his implied promise. More important still, I could see that everything he had said was true: that it might prove disastrous for me as well as embarrassing to the Foundation if they were to grant me a Fellowship. Yet I still couldn't go along with his suggestion. To do so, I argued, would, no matter how we disguised our actions, be little short of unconditional surrender to McCarthyism. Nor was I much impressed by the secretary's pointing out, at this juncture, that the Foundation planned to award a Fellowship to an avowed Communist who had publicly recanted and declared in print how misguided he had been. The granting of such a Fellowship, it seemed to me, merely constituted another form of surrender—a way for the Foundation to salve its liberal conscience while it placated its liberal adherents and gave in to McCarthy pressure.

Nevertheless, as I look back now, I find it difficult to understand why, once I had expressed my views, I could not accept the secretary's suggestion; why, in an effort to lend weight to my refusal, I enlisted the help of my liberal friends. Heilman aided me in every way he could, as did Stull Holt of the Washington history department and numerous others, including the West Coast representative of the Guggenheim Foundation, who actually resigned his position as a result of the controversy that developed over my refusal. These men were, of course, acting on principle, and in part at least I was too. But in my case there was more to it than that. Somehow I had come to see McCarthyism as another version of the authoritarianism I had been encountering from childhood on up, and I couldn't bring myself to give in to it—at least not without a fight. Nor could I believe that the Foundation could save itself by giving in. What good, finally, was a Foundation which had to insist that its Fellows pass McCarthy's tests of purity?

ii

The University of Washington, in those days, was certainly no better, from my point of view, than the Guggenheim Foundation. Indeed the University, in its official pronouncements, sounded very much like the *American Mercury*. At least that was my impression at the time, and that impression has been substantiated by Jane Sanders' account of "academic freedom at the University of Washington, 1946-64" in her *Cold War on the Campus* (1979). But Sanders' book also bears out what I myself knew at first hand: that the English department not only refused to succumb to McCarthyism in the University but actually took the lead in resisting it. Time and again Heilman, speaking for the department, challenged the University's restrictions on the hiring of visiting professors, most notably, perhaps, in defense of the department's nomination of Kenneth Burke as a Walker-Ames Lecturer—a nomination that was eventually rescinded by the president of the University and the Board of Regents (September, 1952) but not before Heilman and the executive committee of the department had stated their case in words that left no doubt as to where they themselves stood. "What is finally at stake in the Burke case," they concluded, "is the direction which the University is going to take in doing something about our immediate world." (Sanders, p. 112)

In the spring of 1953, approximately a year after my return from England, I myself came up for tenure, and the department, by a unanimous vote, if I remember correctly, granted me both tenure and promotion to associate professor. Whether or not the vote came before or after J. B. Matthews' article appeared in the *American Mercury* I can no longer recall. Nor do I see any need to check, since I am morally certain that the department would never have paid serious heed to Matthews' charges—although they would have had every right to do so, if they had chosen to worry about my "vulnerability" the way the Guggenheim people did. For the only other professor from the University of Washington named in the Matthews article, Abraham Keller of the French department, had to appear before the

House Un-American Activities Committee under Chairman Harold Velde when it visited Seattle in the spring of 1954. But the English department refused to be intimidated: at or near the very time that the House Un-American Activities Committee held its hearings the department was trying to get a visiting appointment for still another "Red"—Rolfe Humphries: an appointment that the president of the University "refused" when he "discovered that Humphries . . . had been active in support of the Spanish loyalists in the 1930's." (Sanders, p. 125)

The department's granting my tenure at the time and in the way it did I found immensely gratifying for all kinds of reasons, not the least being that I could, with any luck, look forward to continuing on in the manner and in the directions I had been going without having to worry seriously about being so much at odds about so many things with so many people in the department. For their unanimous vote seemed to indicate that however questionable they might, on occasion, find my ideas or attitudes, they were still, after five years, willing to support me in them—not only for the moment but for years to come. By this time I could no longer think of any university as being a heavenly city, and I'm afraid I could no longer think of departments in these terms either. Yet I think I did see the English department as being about as heavenly as an academic department could get. And I still think I was justified in seeing it that way.

Just to be in a department in which people were still sane and for the most part intelligently unafraid, meant a great deal in those McCarthy days. In the rest of the academic world, including many of the corners of it that I knew about at first hand, professors often had reason to go pussyfooting through the works they were teaching to avoid social or political implications that might prove controversial. Otherwise they might lose their jobs. But there was no such repressive atmosphere in Parrington Hall: it remained as free in the early and middle fifties as it had been when I first arrived. The professor I quoted earlier ("In these days one can't be too careful") was referring to the outside McCarthy world, not to Parrington Hall. There one didn't need to be careful at all.

The department did, as in the case of Kenneth Burke, encounter difficulties in securing temporary appointments. Yet it still managed to bring in all kinds of interesting people, including, just to mention those whom I either knew well or came to know well, Alex Comfort, Kenneth Patchen, James Farrell, Kenneth Rexroth, George Woodcock, Irving Howe, Allen Ginsberg, Gary Snyder, and Herbert Read. All these men gave readings or lectures, and two actually taught classes: Howe for a quarter; Woodcock for a full academic year.

Having these men to talk with and argue with, I can now see, meant considerably more to me than I realized at the time—not so much because I learned a great deal from them, although, in certain instances, I undoubtedly did, but because I gained a new confidence in my own critical ideas and perceptions. In this connection my arguments with Irving Howe, extending over the entire summer of 1953, were especially stimulating. Howe's criticism I already knew, and he, with his Marxist (Trotskyite) background, could sympathize, up to a point, with the critical approach I was trying to work out. We even went so far as to set up a plan for collaborating on a book, to be entitled *Under Distant Eyes*, that was to be a collection of critical essays by non-literary writers (*e.g.*, Marx, Trotsky, Freud), the ultimate idea being to show the superiority of their criticism over the technical stuff being turned out by professional critics. It was a great plan—the plan, even the title, was Howe's—but when we got around to trying to write an introduction and commentaries we found, to my sincere regret, that the critical differences between us were too great for collaboration.

iii

My inability to collaborate with Irving Howe, despite my deep respect for his criticism, may be taken as a measure of the intensity that I was bringing to my own critical thinking during those years—in an effort to develop a contextualist aesthetic that would, as I saw it, enable me and others to save fiction (and with it, literature) from all those teachers and critics who were, in my view, either emasculating it or denying it altogether. And while I wasn't naive enough to think that a contextualist aesthetic could, in and of itself, do very much to save fiction, I did believe that, for me, in the critical battles I had to fight in the classroom and in academic journals, the development of such an aesthetic constituted an essential first step; that without it I wouldn't be able to provide the kind of intellectual help students as well as people in general had to have if they were going to withstand the pressures and blandishments of the prevailing schools of criticism—if, in other words, they were going to realize that there was more to fiction than ideology or morality or uplift; more than myth or symbol or evil or unity or form; more even than all these rolled together; and finally that, on the positive side, the "more" was all that really mattered.

I also knew that a number of critics had already said essentially what I was trying to say; that E. M. Forster had perhaps said it best in his *Aspects of the Novel*. (I am speaking now of the time when I did not as yet know Lawrence's criticism very well.) But Forster had said it all so gently, not to say reticently, that he could be, and usually was, dismissed as vague and even sloppy. The second generation of New Critics had begun to dominate not just the academy but the entire literary scene, and they were turning the techniques that Brooks and Warren and Heilman had used, in their own terms at least, as tools of critical discovery, into tools of power and academic promotion. The time had come, I believed, when they had to be challenged— not in the gentle way Forster's *Aspects* still challenged them, but in ways as direct and forceful as critical language would allow.

The other great threats, I believed, came from those who would, in the name of tradition, or "great books," or Americanism, or some authoritarian ideology, try to impose literary standards that tended, in my view, to reduce fiction to ideology or morality—the way Fascist and Russian critics had been reducing it since World War I. And these critics and professors had to be challenged too—as I had already tried to challenge them in my "Novelist as Revolutionary."

At the time I did not think of myself as being alone in my critical views, although, in the way I held them, I essentially was, and would become more so—for the simple reason, once again, that I couldn't make either the allowances or the compromises that are always necessary when one is working with or sharing common aims with others.

Knowing this about myself I had been somewhat reluctant when, at its first meeting in 1950, Conference 12 of the Modern Language Association (made up of analysts and writers and academics interested in discussing the relationships between literature and depth psychology) had "designated me as one of the three members of the Steering Committee which would, it was hoped, continue the organization during future years." Yet, for all my reluctance, I did accept the appointment, and the three of us did, primarily through Leonard F. Manheim's efforts, continue the organization; also we published a mimeographed journal, again primarily through Manheim's efforts, entitled *Literature and Psychology*. For my part I contributed essays to the journal, read papers at the meetings, and took an active part in the early discussions. But it wasn't long before I began to realize that I would have to take a stand against some of the critical theories and practices of the group; and in the meeting of 1952, in giving my paper on *Jane Eyre*, I stressed, according to the minutes of the meeting, "the necessity of a retreat from the position on psychoanalytic criticism heretofore taken by some critics, including certain members of the Conference. Only by a 'desystematization' of our minds from specific Freudian knowledge and its application to literary criticism, and substitution therefore [sic] of a 'Freudian awareness' can we achieve a genuinely contextualistic criticism."

The ensuing arguments Manheim described in *Literature and Psychology* (Feb., 1953) as "one of the liveliest discussions that ever occurred at a Lit-Psych meeting." But as usual—Manheim and I were, by this time, good friends—his words were far too kind: the discussion which he described as lively actually became, at times, quite bitter. And understandably so, for I was not only, as some of the members saw it, denying Freud, I was doing so in terms that denied them their entire critical approach. All this I could see, and in one sense regret. Yet I could also see that I had no alternative; that once again I had to go my own way—as I eventually did by revising and further developing my paper on *Jane Eyre* and publishing it as a contextualist essay under the title "The Critical Relevance of Freudianism" (*Western Review*, Summer, 1956).

I also published a number of other essays during these years in which I tried to develop my contextualist aesthetic still further: "The Genuine and the Counterfeit: A Study in Victorian and Modern Fiction" (*College English*, December, 1956); "Kafka and Octave Mirbeau" (*Accent*, Winter, 1957); "Cozzens vs. Life and Art," (*Northwest Review*, Summer, 1958); and "The Beat and the Dead," which I chose not to publish at that time. In these essays one of my prime concerns was to bring out the disastrous implications of the New Criticism's conception of "form" and "technique"—to show how, in their critical practice, the New Critics were not only misreading serious novels but also, in the process, rendering them indistinguishable from their popular and bestselling counterparts. And they were doing this, I maintained, not because they were imperceptive, but because they had no basis other than technical excellence for making qualitative distinctions—or at least they had no basis which they were prepared to acknowledge. If the test is "well-wroughtness," I argued, how does one distinguish between "The Well Wrought Urn" and the well wrought cliche, the well wrought serious novel and the well wrought soap opera—except through bootleg appeals to tradition or common sense. Of course I knew that there were formalist answers to this dilemma but I also knew, and pointed out, that in practice they were proving ineffectual—as demonstrated by the critical absurdities New Critics perpetrated whenever they were confronted with really high level soap-opera. "Mistaking means for ends, technique for art," I argued in my essay on Cozzens, "these critics are helpless to cope with the new high-level counterfeit, even when they can recognize, or at least sense, its pretentiousness. Hence the uneasiness that runs through their critical acceptance of *By Love Possessed*: their futile efforts, as in the *Kenyon* and *Hudson* reviews, to rationalize this uneasiness in terms of structure and style; their pointing out, for instance, that structurally, *By Love Possessed* falls short of James's *The Ambassadors*—as if that were the prime qualitative difference between the two works."

The significant qualitative differences, I pointed out, went deeper than form or technique. They were, generally speaking, the differences that E. M. Forster had stressed in his devastating analysis of Sir Walter Scott in *Aspects of the Novel*; that Q. D. Leavis had stressed in characterizing the phoniness of the "literary novel" (*e.g.*, *The Forsyte Saga*; *The Bridge of San Luis Rey*) in her *Fiction and the Reading Public* (1939); that Herbert Gold had stressed in his analysis of Herman Wouk and others in his "The New Upper-Middle Soap Opera," (*Hudson Review*, Winter, 1956–57). Going still further I tried to show that the differences these critics were pointing towards characterized a type of fiction which might well be called "counterfeit," in that it used all the techniques, all the effects, that characterized the great novels of the past and present, but used these techniques and effects, not to "illuminate" experience, as the great novels had invariably done, but to deny it, or, more accurately, to "insulate" readers against it. Then, after defining my terms a bit further, I went on to suggest that many novels of the past and present generally considered genuine or even great were really counterfeit (*e.g.*, *The Catcher in the Rye*, which was then enjoying a tremendous vogue); and in my essay on Cozzens, I tried to demonstrate, through close analysis, just what makes a novel with serious pretentions counterfeit.

My essay on the "Genuine and the Counterfeit," the editors of *College English* informed me, stirred up more rebuttals than they had received for some time. The one they published, entitled "Rebuttal: Art and Counterfeit Art" by Alan Donagan and Martin Steinman, Jr., I found terribly discouraging, since it mistook the entire nature and substance of my argument and ended up saying that I hadn't proved what I had not, in any case, been attempting to prove. Indeed the ultimate effect of the rebuttal was to convince me that there was no way I could effectively communicate with Donagan and Steinman at all, short of abandoning my entire approach and accepting theirs.

John C. Sherwood's rebuttal to my essay on Cozzens ("Burns vs. Cozzens: the Defense," *Northwest Review*, Fall–Winter, 1958) I also found discouraging, and for much the same reason. Nevertheless I did answer it, in a separate essay entitled, "Reiterations," in which I tried once again to clarify my critical position, but without much hope of success. I quote my concluding paragraphs to "Reiterations" not for their intrinsic value, sound as I think they still are, but for what they reveal about my own state of mind at that time:

> Likewise ineffectual are Dr. Sherwood's comparative arguments, since if I accept them they tend to prove, not that *By Love Possessed* is genuine, but that *Lord Jim*, *Nostromo*, and *Absalom, Absalom!* are counterfeit—which of course they are not. Dr. Sherwood has mistaken outward similarities in theme, form, and technique for qualitative likenesses; either that or he has lapsed into the state of the "ordinary reader" he describes earlier—the reader who feels only "generalized human sympathy" when reading the novels of Dickens, Hardy, and Faulkner: "Far from unsettling, such works may comfort the ordinary reader by allowing him to feel superior to the decadents that inhabit them."

> That serious fiction may be so read is, alas, all too true, and bears out my contention (stated explicitly in my essay) that most present-day readers, instead of rejecting serious fiction, in self-defense emasculate it—the way John Lydenberg (on whom Dr. Sherwood leans for critical support) emasculates it in his "Cozzens and the Critics." "The extremes of modern fiction," Lydenberg declares, "do not represent a real danger to *us*." After all, Benjy *is* an idiot, and Quentin a schizophrenic; K *is* living in a nightmare; the world of 1984 *has* been totally transformed." On the basis of these remarks I should say that Lydenberg and the readers he represents are incapable of responding to any form of serious art. Confronted with such readers and critics,

what can the serious novelist do except ignore them, or hope that, by some miracle, they can develop a sense of life that will permit them to realize the connections between life and art?

The final question I raised on behalf of the serious novelist I was also, at this point, raising for myself. It wasn't that I thought of myself as being alone in my dismissal of Cozzens: Irving Howe had written a far more scathing criticism of *By Love Possessed* (*The New Republic*, January 20, 1958). Nevertheless I was beginning to think that my own version of contextualism would never be acceptable to more than a very few of the critics and professors I was trying to reach. It threatened too many vested interests in too many ways. Yet I couldn't temporize or compromise. I just didn't know how—even when, as in the study of Kerouac's novels which I undertook in 1959, I found my own vested interests threatened. My sympathy with the Beats went all the way back to Berkeley, when the movement was called the Berkeley Renaissance. Since that time I had continued to see and talk with Kenneth Rexroth and others, and, more recently, Allen Ginsberg, whom I came to know quite well during the summer he spent in Seattle (1955). Ginsberg admired Celine every bit as much as I did, and in talking about what Celine had meant to him as a poet went on to explain that his friend Jack Kerouac owed even more to Celine than he himself did. That was how I first became interested in Kerouac, and why I began reading him with such high hopes—only to discover, once I got into *On the Road*, that it seemed much closer to Cozzens than to Celine; that, consequently, I had an obligation to begin my criticism by saying so:

> In *On the Road* Jack Kerouac became the fictional spokesman for the beats in much the same sense and for much the same reasons that James Gould Cozzens, in *By Love Possessed*, became the fictional spokesman for their conservative counterparts. Both novels have, as their heroes, father-figures embodying the ultimate virtues and power of the authors' respective ideals. And these father-figures assume the burdens, not merely of the other characters in the novels, but of the readers as well, finally to lead

them, along with the characters, through the forms of absolution appropriate to the authors' respective ideals. Just as Winner serves to justify the fears and insecurities of our gray-flannel literati, by making their quiet Americanism appear tough-minded and heroic, so Moriarty justifies the fears and insecurities of the beats, by making their nerve-end responses appear joyous and human.

This is why the criticism of the two novels has tended to follow partisan lines—lines so tightly drawn that it is difficult to show . . . that Kerouac's *On the Road*, considered as a novel rather than as beat scripture, represents . . . more than a reverse fictional image of the Cozzens formulas.

I say this reluctantly, and after much soul-searching, for my sympathies are wholly with Kerouac, and with his efforts to write a fictional *Howl*.

I never completed the criticism, nor did I publish what I did complete until some ten years later. Partly I didn't want to risk being identified with those who were then attacking the Beats, but mainly I was discouraged by the prospect of trying to communicate with readers who could not grant my critical premises—who could only, wittingly or unwittingly, try to force me into compromises that would render everything I was trying to say innocuous, and therefore meaningless. And while I also knew, at first hand, that all professors and critics weren't like that, I still felt terribly discouraged.

iv

Yet if I felt terribly discouraged by the reception accorded my critical writing I felt terribly encouraged by what was going on in my classes. The critical battles that I had been trying to fight on paper, I had, since my return from England, been introducing more and more directly into my undergraduate as well as my graduate classes—at first rather tentatively; then, as the students seemed responsive, more and more directly.

The great majority of the undergraduate students, once I introduced them to the dramatic format I had worked out, and made it clear that I could be challenged, even resisted, were not the least daunted by the contextualist arguments which I set forth in each class at the beginning of each quarter: for the novelist as revolutionary; for myself as a revolutionary at second hand; for the critical relevance of Freudianism; for the genuine against the counterfeit; for the connections between the world of the novels and the students' own world—connections which would, I stressed, oblige them to see everyone naked and be as naked themselves. Inevitably a few students would be scandalized: one girl, I recall, remarked that she wasn't going to undress for any professor, and proceeded to drop the course. A few others might bristle at my Freudianism, or at my concept of revolutionary irresponsibility. Then they too might drop. But most of the students, unlike the professors and critics with whom I had been contending in the journals, were quite willing to grant me the basic premises of my contextualist approach.

The point of this comparison is not, of course, to ascribe superior powers or virtues to the students. My point is only that the students were not yet burdened with vested interests, or with literary traditions, or with worries about prestige or power. They weren't even, in those days, burdened with worries about grades, or careers—or at least their worries had not taken on the character they have today. In the liberal arts programs at Washington, and more especially in English, there were few required courses. The students were for the most part free to shop around and take whatever courses struck their fancy, with little thought for how those courses might contribute to what are now referred to as "career objectives." It therefore followed, in the courses themselves, that they were free to respond to any critical approach which they found, for whatever reasons, interesting. Nor were they always very particular in their reasons. On one occasion, when a young friend of mine happened to be attending one of the opening sessions in a class I was teaching in the modern novel, the student sitting next to her wanted to know if she had any idea of what I was getting at in all my talk about Freud and revolution and nakedness. And when she said, "Yes, I think so," he quickly responded, "Well, I don't, but it's sure different from any other English class I've had, and maybe something will come of it."

Although the student's remarks may not sound very promising, they were all that I could reasonably expect. If some students were more enthusiastic in their initial responses, that was all to the good. But in the opening sessions of my classes I wasn't asking for, and certainly wasn't getting, very much enthusiastic understanding. That usually came later, after detailed discussion of one or more novels had enabled me to demonstrate just how the novels themselves tended to bear out the theories I had presented at the outset. The great danger, of course, was that I would, by seeking to relate the students' readings of the novels to my theoretical approach, turn my approach into a kind of intellectual cookie-cutter—the way, for example, the Freudian critics I quarreled with were, in my view, fitting literature to Freudian patterns. Contextualism did not, however, lend itself to such an application. It was not, in the first place, a unified philosophy. Indeed my version of it could hardly be called a philosophy at all—except in the sense that it embodied a fairly consistent attitude towards art and experience. Nevertheless I took every precaution to avoid imposing the theory on the fiction, to the point of leaning over backwards in my efforts to do justice to other critical points of view.

In most respects my efforts were, I believe, successful, or as successful as such efforts can very well be. I took the position that every critic has an approach, a philosophy, whether or not he is willing or able to acknowledge it. He has to stand somewhere in reading a novel, or viewing a work of art; he can't, as reader or viewer, be God. He can bounce around and try to convince himself that he is nowhere because he refuses to acknowledge that he is anywhere, but he is merely playing ostrich. And since he has to be somewhere, I argued, it's better for him to know where he is. Then he can talk or write intelligently about his perceptions, even to those who don't share his position. For if they know where he is in relation to where they are they can make allowances for his perspective that will enable them to understand, in a general way at least, what he is saying.

In this sense, I pointed out, I could understand T. S. Eliot's evil far better than I could Brooks and Warren's. In Eliot's dismissal of Hardy and Lawrence, for example, there is no mistaking what he means by evil. He gives both lower and upper case definitions:

> I was [in a previous lecture] . . . concerned with illustrating the limiting and crippling effect of a separation from tradition and orthodoxy upon certain writers. . . . Here I am concerned with the intrusion of the *diabolic* into modern literature in consequence of the same lamentable state of affairs; . . . I am afraid that even if you can entertain the notion of a positive power for evil working through human agency, you may still have a very inaccurate notion of what Evil is, and will find it difficult to believe that it may operate through men of genius of the most excellent character. I doubt whether what I am saying can convey very much to anyone for whom the doctrine of Original Sin is not a very real and tremendous thing.

If all critics could be so forthright, I argued, criticism wouldn't be nearly so confused or so confusing.

For my part I tried to be equally forthright, and I believe I did, in my undergraduate classes, manage to combine theory with practice in such a way as to deepen, without restricting, their responses to the novels. But in the process I ran into unforeseen consequences, since I found it impossible to effect the combination without having my theory of fiction turn into a theory of life. I didn't want that to happen, or at least I didn't want it to happen in the way it often did happen. For I had no lust for power, no desire to become some kind of guru. The most I wanted to do was provide the students with a way of understanding fiction that was also, as I believed it had to be, a way of understanding life in all its dismaying complexity. Then, if they wanted to accept that way, rather than one of the other ways available, they could do so. But I wouldn't force them. They could, if they wished, choose the way of T. S. Eliot, or F. R. Leavis, or Brooks and Warren, or anyone else who made critical sense. It wasn't an empty gesture on my part: some students did make one or another of these choices and I did my level best to honor them.

Yet if I wasn't forcing I was inevitably persuading. I couldn't do anything else. In consciously setting myself up as the teacher as revolutionary, committed to helping the students who wished to follow the novelist as revolutionary wherever he might lead, I had, in effect, committed myself to going places with students that teachers do not ordinarily go. In asking them to be naked I had to be naked too; or more accurately, I had to be naked first, since I, as the teacher, couldn't ask them to do what I had not yet done. I couldn't, in other words, ask them to make connections I hadn't made. Their world was also my world, their difficulties my difficulties, and if they were going to connect the world of the novels with their world, I had to acknowledge the same or similar connections. I couldn't stand apart and watch.

I am speaking as if these were my conscious decisions, arrived at through reasoning—as, to a large extent they were. But I must also acknowledge that, once I placed myself in the position of the teacher as revolutionary, I really didn't have much choice. The students would never have permitted me to stand apart, even if I had wanted to. How could they—if the everyday world they lived in really was the way the novelists were showing it to be? If there really was no way that individuals could be part of society and its institutions and still maintain their individuality, no matter how liberal the society and its institutions? If, more specifically, there really was no way that a person could even vote without surrendering to the system? In confronting these questions, and the novelist's implied answers, the students had to ask: what do we do? What alternative do we have? Questions which had, as their corollary: what do you do? What alternative do you have?

To my own credit I can honestly say that I never relished these questions; never, to the best of my knowledge, used them for purposes of self-aggrandizement. Yet I had to answer them as intelligently and as discreetly as I could, always prefacing my answers with a reminder that contextualism was a theory of crit-

icism, not a theory of life; that serious novels rarely provided us
with answers to the human dilemmas they presented; that each
of us had to work out his own answers in relation to his own
situation and abilities; that some individuals—and here I was
offering the kind of personal observation or reminiscence I
preferred to use—could even maintain their individuality
through long stretches in the navy; that one man I knew, a good
friend who had been a student of mine and was now a professor,
had spent eleven years in the navy, and come out a more confirmed conscientious objector than he had been when he was
drafted.

Ultimately, however, I had to acknowledge my own feelings
and attitudes on many questions that I would have preferred to
avoid, drawing the line only when I thought the questions or
comments were more appropriate to the columns of Dorothy
Dix (the Dear Abby of the time) than to intellectual discussion
in a classroom. It was a fine line I was trying to follow: I recall,
for instance, trying to answer one student's comments when she
pointed out that the way we were reading D. H. Lawrence a
girl's only answer was to marry Lawrence, or, since he was dead,
me. The way she phrased her comment it actually did have serious implications, and it provided me with an opportunity to define the necessary limits of my own involvement—limits that I
scrupulously adhered to, even when, as sometimes happened,
especially in conferences, students would challenge me to act
out what, according to them, I had been preaching. Then if
they charged me with being an intellectual phony, which a few
of them did, I simply had to accept the charge.

Even so, Alex Comfort, who visited several of my classes in
the late fifties, had quite severe things to say about them. What
I was doing in the classroom, he maintained, amounted to "in-
complete analysis," and could be really quite dangerous, since I
was, as he saw it, functioning as analyst rather than teacher,
and in the process was bringing the students to the point of seeing how desperate their own situations were, then leaving them
to work their own way out of their dilemmas as best they could,
with only a few shreds of humanistic philosophy to guide them.

While I had to acknowledge an element of truth in this observation, I still maintained, in talking with Comfort, that, dangerous as the process might be, it was really the best if not the only way to help the students to a full understanding of the novels—and, through the novels, of themselves and the world they lived in.

Whether or not I was right, and I still think that I was, the ultimate effect of my teaching as I did was to give my contextualism a dimension that I had not originally intended. It became for some students what it had long been for me—a way of trying to think and read and write and live that would enable them to survive and grow, as individuals, in a world that seemed bent on institutionalizing them. For these students I became, not exactly a hero and certainly not a leader (although I think I might, if I had chosen, have become both) but a professor who was also a kind of intellectual father. The more enthusiastic students took class after class with me, and a number went on to graduate school, where they continued to work with me right on through their Ph.D. theses.

At long last I had become the undergraduate teacher that, from Miami onwards, I had been trying to become. And I felt happy and fulfilled—though by no means complacent. For I could never overcome the anguish I felt at having to be responsible, even at second hand, for the pain and disillusionment that I so often heard in the students' voices or saw written on their faces. At these times I tried to tell myself that I shouldn't be sentimental, that the students were merely going through a process that I had gone through, that every reader of serious fiction had to go through. It was, I tried to remind myself, neither more nor less than the process which I had described so confidently, with D. H. Lawrence's help, in my "Cozzens vs. Life and Art":

> I dwell on this passage [from *The Rainbow*] because it demonstrates a crucial point: that art, if it is genuine, can never be pretty or comforting, can never leave us secure in our protective rationalizations. It must always shock or hurt, in the sense that

Lawrence himself explains in "The Morality of the Novel": "A new relatedness hurts somewhat in the attaining; and will always hurt. So life will always hurt. Because real voluptuousness lies in reenacting old relationships, and at the best, getting an alcoholic sort of pleasure out of it, slightly depraving . . . Obviously, to read a really new novel will *always* hurt, to some extent. There will always be resistance. The same with new pictures, new music. You may judge of their reality by the fact that they do arouse a certain resistance, and compel, at length, a certain acquiescence."

But it was one thing to assume responsibility for the "hurt" in print; quite another to assume responsibility for it in the classroom.

I also tried to assuage my doubts by telling myself that students were wonderfully resilient; that I had never forced them, never enticed them; that I was, in any event, leaving them all kinds of ways out—in case they decided, at any time, that they didn't want anything more to do with me or contextualism or serious fiction. One girl, after hearing me quote Dorothy Dix's description of an ideal wife (I often quoted Dorothy Dix) stopped by after class to inform me that she was about to be married, that she knew her husband wanted her to be a Dorothy Dix wife, and that she was prepared to be what he wanted her to be. So why should she read stories that were going to make her unhappy with her chosen lot? And I had to agree: there really was no reason for her to read serious fiction when she was certain that it would only make her unhappy in her ultimate commitments.

For students to read the way I was asking them to read they had to feel free to change their outlooks—even their lives. Otherwise the connections I was asking them to make would become a meaningless torture, my classes little better than torture chambers. If the time ever came when, in order to survive, they really did have to chain themselves, body and mind, to their society and its institutions, then they would, I acknowledged, have to reject serious fiction out of hand. And I would, as a teacher, have to reject it with them. But till that time came, I couldn't see that I had any alternative but to carry on—in the hope that my feelings of sympathy for the students might help me overcome the dangers inherent in what I was attempting.

v

By the time I became really active in graduate teaching, in the early fifties, I already had a considerable following among the graduate students—a ready-made following, so to speak, since a number of my enthusiastic undergraduates had continued on into graduate school, where they worked with me all through their course work and exams and theses, a few for as long as six or seven years. All through the fifties, therefore, I had the interest and support of a dedicated group of students who were themselves committed to my critical views, and who, over the years, helped to persuade many other graduate students, particularly those coming in from other universities, to take my classes and to give my contextualist approach to literature serious consideration.

At times, I must admit, the students' enthusiasm far outran their good sense, notably when, in one or another of my colleagues' seminars, they would try to introduce my theories or ideas at completely inopportune moments—as, for instance, when one of them pointed out, in the first meeting of a seminar on modern fiction, that several of the novels they were being asked to read were, according to Wayne Burns, "counterfeit." There were innumerable other instances too, including one in which a student even went so far, on his Ph.D. exam, as to refuse to discuss the "structure" of a given work—on the ground that, as a contextualist, he had no obligation to do so. Yet in this as in all such instances my colleagues managed to exonerate me personally, however much they may have been upset by the students, since I think they knew—or, if they didn't know, my close friends in the department eventually persuaded them— that I did not, in any sense, condone antics of this kind; that I deplored not only the antics themselves but the partisan spirit which gave rise to them. Unless I am mistaken, then, the worst that was said about me around the department during those years went something like this: Burns himself isn't so bad; it's what he does to his students.

For the tolerance my colleagues thus extended to me personally I was, of course, grateful. But at the same time I could see that it was double-edged; that even as it excused me as a scholar and a man it raised serious questions about me as a teacher—or, what amounts to the same thing, it raised serious questions about the effects of my teaching. This too, I could understand: I could see clearly enough that however much respect I showed my colleagues, however carefully I presented my contextualist approach, it invariably encouraged the students who accepted it to see themselves in an embattled position—a position in which they felt obliged to defend their "true" and "radical" and "human" approach against what they looked upon as the institutionalized stuffiness of the department. And while I did everything I could to counter these attitudes—by pointing out that no English department could be more free, more open, more alive; that no other department would give them the freedom of expression they were enjoying; that at Berkeley, for instance, my deviations, and theirs, would simply not be tolerated—my efforts were never entirely successful. The students who accepted my approach could not see why, if the professors in the department were all that great, the freedom I spoke of could not be exercised in all their classes, on all their exams, from *Beowulf* to Joyce. Nor did it help much for me to counter this argument by pointing out that all scholars and critics did not see difference and conflict as desirable or even tolerable.

In any event, whatever the arguments or admonitions I gave the students, I could never escape the effects of my own example, never deny the tendentious position I myself felt obliged to take in my classes in order to justify the more controversial aspects of my own critical views. Always, in presenting my case, I tried to be rigorously fair to other points of view, but fairness is one thing, zeal another, and all my zeal went into the presentation of my own approach. Not just because it was mine (via Stephen Pepper and John Dewey and countless others) but because I honestly believed that it could provide a way of understanding and teaching literature that would open up new and significant possibilities for any graduate student who could accept its premises.

Outwardly there were still no great differences between my graduate and undergraduate classes—except that, in the graduate classes, I expected the students to read more, to explore the works and the critical issues more deeply and fully. But I could sense more subtle differences, especially in my atttitude towards the students, which made for a still further breakdown of the usual barriers which separate teacher from student. For in my graduate classes, now for the most part made up of students whom I knew fairly well, I no longer had the feeling that my words might have dangerous consequences. The students were, many of them, as old or older in years and experience than I was; they were, or I believed they were, fully capable of rejecting both me and my critical views any time they chose. Certainly they were free to do so, since, on the graduate level, I taught no required courses, and there were other professors in the department who taught courses in criticism and in Victorian and modern fiction. On my side, therefore, I could go as far as my perceptions would take me. And many of the students responded in kind—to discover in contextualism what they had been unable to find in the criticism they had previously encountered.

Once I had led these students to accept my critical views and, perhaps more importantly, once I had infected them with my zeal, I could not, in conscience, abandon them—even when, in their enthusiasm, a few of them began to form themselves into a loosely knit group which had many of the qualities of a sect. While I could, as in the instances I have noted, disavow students' sectarian proclivities, I could not disavow my connection with the students themselves. If, for example, a graduate student said something silly or sectarian in the name of contextualism there was very little I could do beyond expressing my dismay and pointing out the implications of his remarks. I could not, without becoming sectarian myself, tell him he was hopeless, and should be drummed out of the contextualist critical corps. Nor could I deny a graduate student my attention if he wanted to discuss his contextualist interpretation of some work he was reading on his own, or in another class, or, since most of the graduate students in the group were also TA's, some work he was discussing in one of his own classes.

By the mid fifties, therefore, I had developed closer relationships with a number of graduate students than with all but a few of my colleagues—not because I had set out to cultivate graduate students, in the hope of building up a following among them, but rather because my approach to art, and literature, and life had a stronger appeal for them than it could possibly have for my colleagues, who were, understandably, committed to their own views, their own work. Then, as I myself came to feel more and more isolated in my critical position, on a professional level, I turned more and more to sympathetic graduate students for intellectual stimulation and support. After all they were reading much of what I was reading, and they were willing, even anxious, to talk for hours on end about the contextualist questions that most concerned me—something I could hardly expect even my closest friends on the faculty to do.

I knew, of course, that my close relationships with the graduate students were at times misunderstood—most drastically by a few of my more nervous colleagues who became convinced that I had ulterior motives, that I was cultivating the students in order to gain popularity, or to build up a following which would give me power in the department. One assistant professor, after leaving the department to go to another university, actually went so far as to write a novel in which he cast me as the villainous professor bent on bringing graduate students under my control for all kinds of nefarious purposes—my ultimate aim being, according to the novel, to effect a coup in which I would unseat the chairman and take over the department and eventually the University. Absurd as I knew the novel to be I felt relieved when I later heard that it had little if any chance of being published—in part because the villainous professor lacked credibility. As well he might, in so far as he bore any resemblance to me, for power, in the sense of directing or controlling activities in the department or the University, either directly or indirectly, had no appeal to me whatsoever. A fact which I think nearly everyone in the department recognized. If they at times found my zeal as a teacher naive or misguided they nevertheless acknowledged that it was genuine, and made whatever allowances for it they could.

Quite possibly I am presenting a rosier picture of my position in the department than the facts, if they were available, would warrant. But I don't really think so, since the department continued to be so amazingly free and permissive. In any event I do know that I never received a direct word of censure from Heilman or any of the senior professors in the department. Nor did I encounter any serious difficulties with my colleagues over the theses I supervised.

vi

In those days at Washington the department appointed a committee of three to supervise each graduate student's Ph.D. thesis, although, in practice, the student himself chose the chairman of his committee, who then supervised the writing of the thesis, with the other two members serving as consultants who ordinarily had little to do with the thesis until it was submitted to them in completed form. In effect, therefore, the student and his chairman (or, as I preferred to think of it, his advisor or supervisor) were essentially on their own in a one to one relationship throughout the actual writing of the thesis—an arrangement that, from the very first, I found congenial. And as I became more deeply involved in my work as an advisor, I began to realize that it was taking on greater meaning for me than I had imagined it could—that it was, in fact, giving me a sense of shared difficulty and accomplishment that I had never experienced in my classroom teaching. Just helping another individual to achieve a full realization of his critical understanding can be a satisfying experience in itself; and when, as in several of the theses I supervised during these years, the other individual's perceptions differ from or go beyond the teacher's, the experience can take the teacher into creative realms which he could never reach on his own.

One such thesis was that of the late James Wright, the poet, entitled *The Comic Imagination of the Young Dickens* (1959)—a strikingly original critical study which should long since have been published. Although Wright had taken one of my seminars on Dickens in 1956, and had written a long term paper on *Martin Chuzzlewit*, he did not begin serious work on the thesis until after he left Seattle, in the fall of 1957, to teach at the University of Minnesota; and I am therefore fortunate enough to have, in a series of letters covering the period from September, 1957, to January, 1959, Wright's detailed account of his thoughts and feelings from the time he first began to formulate the thesis until he completed the final chapter.

To do justice to this account I should quote Wright's letters at length. But that is clearly impossible, since the individual letters sometimes run to two or three thousand words. The best I can do is to provide a few excerpts, beginning with the letter of November 30, 1957, in which, after confessing that the only thing he "can actually write down on paper is verse," Wright goes on to discuss everything from his reading for the thesis to his own deepest feelings of "exile and revolt":

> I rise early and read like hell—all kinds of nutty, sinful stuff: Shaw, Tolstoy, George Gissing, Shakespeare, Sterne: and these are my Dickens critics!
>
> What I mean is that I've been through the Dickens shelves in the Univ. of Minn. library (my God, you ought to see them, they would startle Dickens himself), and I've even looked through the whole *Dickensian*, and yet the only useful critics I can find are all of them utterly strange and unlikely. I know you won't mind unorthodox critics on Dickens in my essays (and when, Oh for Christes sake, when will those essays be written?) . . .
>
> I also found the perfect image of the Dickensian imagination

in *Don Quixote*. I don't know why it never occurred to me before, but do you remember that comic passage where Sancho tells the story of the man ferrying the hundred goats across the stream one by one (with full detailed description of each goat and each ferrying trip) and is interrupted by Don Quixote with the demand that he say simply that all hundred goats were ferried across? The joke is that a storyteller ought to get to the point. But Dickens is backwards from this. If we conceive his plots as the "point," then he never gets to it; and, in the process of evading it, he forgets, and makes us forget, the other side of the stream, and he forgets what he wanted to do there; he is so delighted with his goats—the brown goats, the green goats, the old goats without beards, the young female goats that need shaves, the ferryman's plastic leg, and, perhaps most exciting of all, with the ferryman's second cousin's sister-in-law's goiter. Anyway, I have conceived the grand strategy of retelling the story as I found it in *Don Quixote* and using it as a critical metaphor. What do you think? . . .

I just remembered another wonderful Dickens thing (disguised) which I found: in one of his essays on art (I'll look it up later), Tolstoy tells us how to read a great book. The whole passage is striking and true. No wonder Tolstoy liked Dickens so much. Incidentally, your seminar method of finding the true Dickens criticism is working (I hope). I just read the great novels, and the great novelists on one another (like Gorky's *Reminiscences of Tolstoy*, a book by God that would *make your hair stand up on end and dance Dixie*), and, if those writers are post-Dickens, they make some comment on him sooner or later. Sometimes, as in the case of Sterne and Cervantes, they comment on Dickens even before he was born. Has anyone ever studied *Tristram Shandy* as a work of literary criticism? It's loaded. . . .

. . . the people in this town have been nice to me, and I hate the town like death. I am so unutterably miserable in the midwest that I am numb for all of every day except in the very early morning hours, when I read and write. I'm afraid to speak of this, yet I must. I'm afraid, because I can't seem to make anyone understand the dreadful, practically subconscious, effect that the landscape of a town makes on me. I was so happy in Seattle that I almost felt sinful about it—a sure sign of happiness. I think often how I would like to ask Leggett or Heilman to let me come back to Washington; but I can't write the appropriate letter, because I realize that they would say no, that they would say I am just suffering from the graduate student's lonely neurosis during the first year away from the womb of his native graduate school. So it seems impossible to escape. Will you please keep this in mind, Wayne? I've not said this to anyone, because it sounds so silly in words: but—everything I write in this town seems a fight against Nature, and I'm sick of fighting Nature. I fought it till I escaped from the Ohio Valley, and I was in harmony with it in Seattle. I achieved a great amount of work there, and I could do it again. I've written some verses here; but I always have the feeling that I'm trying in despair to nourish myself from within in defense against this exile. During my years of study at Washington, I labored with joy, and I produced, I got my work done. I did well, and in addition to graduate work I wrote a book. Yet it seems that my simply having attended Washington was a crime for which I have to be punished by exile. Please don't laugh at my melodramatic tone. These are the terms in which my life presents itself to me all the time. . . .

To get to something perhaps amusing, I've been corresponding with my best student at Washington, a talented young person (God, I feel about a thousand years old) named Miss Sonjia Urseth. I sent her a copy of the new poem called "All the Beautiful Are Blameless," and asked her to give it to you. I also wanted her to meet you . . . I hope she succeeds pretty soon. I think she needs to talk very much with someone like you. You don't mind, do you?

In the months that followed, Wright managed to throw off his feelings of depression, although he still could not get started on the thesis. Then on June 25, 1958, he wrote:

Tomorrow morning I am going to send you chapter one. It is called "In Sancho's Country" for reasons which, I am hopefully convinced, will become clear when you begin to read it. All I need to say at this time, I think, is that the first chapter is two things: first, it is a long and careful (though at the same time, curiously, it is wild) argument in favor of what I am calling Critical Irreverence, and an explanation of my idea that, though a critic ought to be irreverent toward his text and toward other critics in the case of every great writer, Dickens is a great writer who by his very nature requires a constantly new and irreverent reading; second, it is a slow and, again, careful approach toward a workable definition of Dickens' comic imagination. . . .

At the moment, I shudder to confess that chapter one, as it stands in the form which I am sending you, is pretty long. Please don't be angry: it is sixty-six pages. . . . I admire nothing in critical prose so much as I admire brevity and precision; and what an irony it is to realize, even at the moment of writing, how I myself can attain precision, if I ever do, only by a kind of encircling ecstasy of long sentences and arguments. Things flood into my mind, and the struggle to tame them long enough to get them down on the paper is not a pain but a joy. That joy is my enemy, I suppose.

I think, at least I hope, that the argument will be clear, even if it seems somewhat drawn-out. . . .

Having given a general definition of the Dickensian comic imagination (a definition which I announce as an *instrument of discovery*, necessary in the light of the frequently disastrous attempts of readers and critics to account for the whole of Dickens), and having mentioned in addition the authors (both critics and novelists, sometimes both) from whom I have partially drawn my definition, I am going to discuss various phases of that comic imagination throughout the first six novels. . . .

Finally, I will test my whole *instrument of discovery* on the novel which is simultaneously the greatest of Dickens' early novels, the crisis in his conscious attitude toward society both mid-Victorian and modern, the most haphazardly written, and yet the most coherently constructed of his books up to 1844, the book in which (I am arguing this pugnaciously and in detail) Dickens is a poet according to any good definition known to me, including that of Philip-Rahv-out-of-Christopher-Caudwell-and-Katherine-Ann-Porter. In short, the climactic and, I pray to God, fulfilling chapter will deal with the *whole* (not just a phase) of *Martin Chuzzlewit*. The final chapter, in other words, will be at once an illustration of the *instrument of discovery* described in chapter one, a test of its validity, and (the most important aim) an attempt to reveal, as fully as I am critically and imaginatively capable of revealing, what the novel *is*, what it is *about*, and what it is worth.

It is a comic epic in prose (the one Fielding didn't write); it is
an illumination of Tyranny, and it is set in Hell; and, in so far as
it is a successful work of fictional art, it is a subversive book, one
of the main modern documents in the analysis and exposure of
tyranny (Mill's "On Liberty" is another, and I am using this
essay in a nutty but, I think, valid way).

But I have a hell of a time tearing my mind away from
Chuzzlewit, which I adore. To me, the conclusive proof that the
character Sir John Falstaff had no mortal prototype is the fact
that, had Falstaff lived, he would have written the works of
Dickens; and, as we know, Dickens' early novels were not written by Falstaff, but by Maria Edgeworth.

Wayne, don't be annoyed. I'm just fooling around by way of
telling you that I'm sending the revised first chapter tomorrow.
It ought to speak for itself.

The chapter did speak for itself; as did all of the succeeding
chapters. Wright completed the thesis over Christmas vacation
(1958), while he was still working on the manuscript of his *Saint
Judas* as well as translations of Lorca, Neruda, Georg Trakl, and
Jorge Guillen; and in his letter of January 7, 1959, after acknowledging the date of his final exam, (January 30, 1959), he
wrote with Dickensian ebullience of his plans for the days he
would be in Seattle, never stopping until he reached the seventh
stage of his triumphant homecoming:

7. Conversation: I want to see Dawson, and Doheny, and
Larry Lawrence, and you and Joan, and the Lawyers (are they
there, and okay?), and, in short, all the mortal enemies of blue-
stockingism. And I want to talk with a couple of former
students. Can I do this in your office? there are, believe it or not,
kids in the world who trust me, and who make me believe in myself as a man and as a writer. I would far rather be true to them
than to some middle-aged vision of myself as the local returning
poete.

AND   WAIT   TILL   YOU   HEAR   ME   DELIVER
PECKSNIFF'S AFTER* DINNER SPEECH ON DIGESTION.
I used it at the Lockwood Memorial Library in Buffalo, and
Wellesley. What a time!

Did you see the hysterical academic attack on you in a recent COLLEGE ENGLISH? Let's go over that, and also over the thing by what's his name in the NORTHWEST REVIEW. (By the way, I'm to be in BEST ARTICLES AND STORIES AGAYNE TOO: maybe we'll be making it together, as Allen Ginsberg says, under the hip moon.)

I'm loaded with Chinese, and Japanese, and Spanish, and German, and French. I feel like a misguided Dago in Munich, burrowing thru the alimentary canal of Peru with nothing on but my underwear. Did you ever hear of Cesar Vallejo? Ah, poetry! WAIT TILL YOU SEE THE SECOND ISSUE OF *THE FIFTIES*. It's beat!

> Love to Joan and you, and, my God, I'm so happy and relieved! I really believe in this thesis, and I pray for it, and for all of us: Lib, and Franz, and Marsh, and me. We can't starve now! Not with this great family finding itself at home at last, and me writing books like a cement-mixer!

Dickens himself could hardly have provided a happier ending. It was wonderful, as Wright's advisor, to see him overcome his feelings of exile and revolt through genuine creative achievement, and equally wonderful to share his unabashed enjoyment of that achievement. And while none of the other graduate students whom I advised during those years came through their trials and tribulations in quite the same way, or with quite the same flair, there was always, for me, much the same sense of shared intellectual adventure and accompishment.

To hardened graduate professors it may seem at this point as if I have, in looking back, recalled only my work with a few unusual students and forgotten the tedium and frustration of advising students who either had no ideas of their own or could not trust the ideas they did have and consequently had to be pushed from one paragraph to another through an entire thesis.

But the way things worked out students of this latter type never chose to work with me. Some of them, I know, found me and my contextualist approach totally unacceptable; others, I believe, felt that I was too controversial and might lead them into trouble. In any event the students who did choose to work with me were of a more independent, more adventurous turn of mind. They accepted my contextualist approach, wholly or in part, but only as a guide, not as a critical blueprint. They were, like Wright, constantly striking out for themselves in directions which, to the best of my knowledge, theses had seldom if ever gone. Trying to help them to realize their perceptions in acceptable scholarly form therefore proved to be every bit as challenging as anything I had attempted in the classroom—and in one sense even more rewarding. For the finished theses were, in my judgment, significant contributions to scholarship and criticism.

6

Bursting the Seams
of Venus's Girdle
(1959–1965)

MY BOOK that started out to be a book on Charles Reade and developed into a study of Victorian authorship (*Charles Reade: A Study in Victorian Authorship*) finally appeared in 1961—after years of struggle with publishers. My struggle, I realize, was not all that different from the struggles other scholars were going through at the time, and if I had been able to survive my ordeal by publishers' fire the way so many of them survived theirs I might still be an active Victorian scholar. But I failed to survive: not because I was more sensitive to publishers' criticisms and rejections but rather, rightly or wrongly, because I came to see the entire process of publishing scholarly books as a negation of scholarship.

My first serious encounter with a publisher came in 1955. In that year, thanks to a Huntington Library Fellowship, I managed to bring the book so close to completion that I submitted my manuscript to Herbert van Thal of Arthur Barker, Ltd. I felt all the more comfortable in doing this because van Thal had been interested in my work on Reade since as early as 1952, and had in fact read a couple of my early chapters with interest and approval. The full-length manuscript, however, proved to be another matter. In his letter of October 29, 1955, van Thal rejected the manuscript out of hand, declaring it a "fearfully dull and long winded" book about "an entirely forgotten figure" which he "cannot see any hope of selling." "As a commercial proposition," he concluded, "it does not stand a chance."

Van Thal's rejection, needless to say, could hardly have been more direct, not to say brutal; and it was all the more disappointing because he had previously been so encouraging. Yet it was also more than a little puzzling, since, after making such a point of having "studied the manuscript very carefully," he went on to dismiss it in terms which suggested that he had failed to read it at all—or, if he had read it, that he had failed to comprehend what I was attempting to do. I knew Reade was an "entirely forgotten figure;" I stressed that fact in the book. I knew, furthermore, that Reade could not be resuscitated; that even though he and many critics of his time considered his novels superior to those of George Eliot and in fact all of his contemporaries except Dickens, which in many respects they are, the novels themselves are at once too Victorian and too wildly eccentric to appeal to modern readers. My aim therefore was not to resuscitate Reade but to use his fictional efforts to show how broad and deep were the main currents of mid-Victorian art and thought which swept Reade and all but a few of his contemporaries, in a few of their novels, into what we now recognize as Victorian stereotypes. Or, put more directly, my aim was to show what mid-Victorian novelists were up against in their efforts to write serious novels—an aim which could be realized more fully through a study of Reade than through any other mid-Victorian because he left such an incredibly voluminous and detailed account of his literary aims and techniques in his Notebooks.

If van Thal had given any indication that he understood all this and then said, "As a commercial proposition it does not stand a chance," I might have been disappointed but I could have acknowledged his verdict as that of a man who knew his trade far better than I did—an acknowledgment that would have been all the easier because I myself had long since recognized that the book probably would not "sell." Any book with "Reade" in the title already had two strikes against it commercially, and my explorations of matters not commonly dealt with in studies of Victorian novelists might very well lead to a third. My hope, a hope that I had expressed to van Thal, though he seemed to have forgotten it, was that some commercial publisher might be willing to take a chance. For I knew that the book, whether it sold or not, explored areas that had never yet been explored, at least in the ways I was trying to explore them, and I believed that it might come to be recognized as a book that opened up new possibilities for the understanding of Victorian fiction.

Although Rinehart, the next commercial publisher I tried, also rejected the manuscript, they did so in terms that I could understand and in a manner which could hardly have been more humane. Claude B. McCaleb, of Rinehart, wrote me on December 20, 1956:

> I found Reade a fascinating person in his own right and agree that you have used him effectively to illuminate a much broader problem. However, I believe that the scope of the work is still too narrow to have much appeal to a commercial publisher. Moreover, I am afraid that the presentation is a bit too scholarly for the so called intelligent layman at whom we would have to direct this book. I may well be wrong. I hope I am. Let's see what some of the people in New York with more experience think.

Then, on January 14, 1957, Frederick S. Cushing wrote me from New York to give me the sad news from both the College editors and the Trade department—along with his regrets and good wishes and a few words of advice:

> As I believe I told you in my recent letter, I have read the manuscript and found it most interesting, not only for the insight into the life of Charles Reade, but also as a study in the creative problems faced by modern authors. During my reading, it became more obvious to me that your study would lend itself

more readily to a University Press than to a more commercial house.

At this point I had to follow Cushing's advice. I knew it was sound, and in any case I could see no realistic alternative. Yet I still felt reluctant because I knew all too well, from the publishing experiences of my academic friends, how difficult it could be to get a book accepted by a university press. And my worst fears were soon realized—in the form of readers' reports that were not all total rejections but from my point of view might as well have been, since the cuts and revisions they suggested were so drastic that I couldn't even consider them. To do so, I firmly believed, would be to abandon the book and write another and inferior one. For better or worse—and I could see at the time it would, from a practical point of view, undoubtedly be worse—I simply could not accept the conditions that any university press would impose.

Once again I was up against the system, and once again I could not bring myself to do what was sensible. Instead I began searching for alternatives. I could, of course, abandon the manuscript altogether; or, a less drastic alternative, I could abandon the manuscript as a book and publish it in a series of scholarly articles. But this plan still seemed too drastic, in that the manuscript was not a series of articles. It was a book, and it made sense only in the form of a book. At this point a friend suggested I try a vanity press, pointing out that some of them were not only quite responsible but also produced quite handsome books, the one drawback, apart from expense, being the fact that even the best of such presses were looked down upon by most academics. This latter consideration I did not take very seriously, since I felt confident that the book, once published, would speak for itself. Nor did my having to subsidize the book out of my personal funds give me serious pause. I would simply have to take out a second mortgage or find some other way to raise the money.

As things worked out, however, I never had to take any such measures. In canvassing the vanity presses I discovered that Bookman Associates, an affiliate of Twayne Publishers, would publish books which they believed to have merit on a share basis—with the author putting up a share of the publishing costs while the press itself assumed the rest of the financial burden. More than that they would guarantee the author the integrity of his manuscript, subject only to nominal supervision from their editors. All I needed then was money. And I managed to secure that through a loan from a local bank and a liberal grant from the Agnes Anderson Fund at the University of Washington.

Bookman Associates then did their best to live up to their contract. They squeezed every word of the manuscript (estimated at 130,000 words) into a book of 360 pages that would, in most respects, bear comparison with the books of commercial presses. Bookman's one serious lapse came when their representative in England somehow failed to distribute review copies to English newspapers and journals—a lapse which prevented the book from being reviewed at all in England, the one place where, despite van Thal's pronouncements, I hoped it might provoke some general interest.

In this country my hopes for any kind of favorable recognition were slim indeed. And it was well for me that they were, since the reviews, with remarkably few exceptions, showed little comprehension of any part of the book—much less the book as a whole. What I was hoping for in the reviews, I should explain, was not lavish praise, pleasant as that might have been, but some recognition of what the book attempted and achieved. To have the book dismissed for not doing what I never intended it to do, what I had, in my introduction, specifically stated it would not attempt to do—that I found really discouraging. It seemed as if the reviewers simply could not refrain from typing the book according to their own preconceptions (as a biography, or the author and his works, or a critical study, or a psychoanalytic case history, or an historical survey) and then faulting it for not living up to their preconceived categories. Or if they did heed the words in the introduction, in which I specifically denied the applicability of such categories, they seemed puzzled or indignant—as if they could not conceive of a book which was trying to do something different.

One reviewer who seemed to be deliberately misrepresenting the book I felt compelled to answer with some vehemence (*Victorian Studies*, March, 1962, pp. 281-282). But the misrepresentations of the other reviewers, I could see, were neither malicious nor spiteful. The book had simply asked more of them than they were able or willing to give. At the same time, however, I could also see that I would never be able or willing to write a scholarly book that such reviewers could accept. And since they seemed to speak for most readers, and, through them, to set the terms for all commercial and scholarly publishing, I could not see that I had any future as a scholarly writer. True, the book had reached a few understanding reviewers (J. P. Pritchard, for example, in the *Oklahoman*, August 26, 1962) along with perhaps more than a few understanding readers. But these people I could communicate with in other and more direct ways—through my teaching and perhaps through critical as distinct from scholarly writing.

ii

In the meantime, while I was going through my personal turmoil in connection with the Reade book, it had been well received in the department, and the University had granted me a full professorship. That I should receive the University's ultimate promotion at the very time when I had determined to abandon scholarly research seemed to me sadly ironical. I knew very well that the promotion was based in large measure on my promise as a publishing scholar, and if I had not been (as Lehman earlier described me) utterly without a sense of institutional sin, I might at least have experienced twinges of guilt—as if I were accepting my professorship under false pretenses. Yet I can honestly say that I never felt the slightest twinge. Nor could I see, given my anarchist perspective, any valid reason why I should. To my way of thinking the University as an institution was neither more nor less than Lionel Trilling declared it to be when he said that, in his time, he never dreamed that the university as an institution was anything but a necessary evil, something that had to be there in order for him and other students to attend a few interesting classes.

In my view, then, my obligations to the University were merely nominal: my real obligations were to the students and the colleagues whom I respected. So long as I did not let them down I could take every advantage of my professorship that it offered. And I could not see that I was letting them down by giving up scholarly research. A few of my close friends in the department would, I knew, be disappointed to learn that I did not intend to follow out the plans I had been so long developing for a book on Dickens, but I also knew that they would understand. As for the students, including the graduate students, published scholarship meant little to them: their interest was in what I brought to the classroom, or to my work with them on their theses. And I had no intention of becoming less of a scholar in either my teaching or my advising. Neither, for that matter, did I intend to become less of a writer—only a different kind of a writer. What I had been unable to accomplish by combining research with criticism, I still hoped I might accomplish in straightforward critical writing. I knew, of course, from the reception accorded my previous critical essays, that my efforts to explain and apply my contextualist theories would never bring me a big reputation. But I had no interest in gaining a reputation, much as I might have enjoyed having one. My interest was in gaining a hearing for my contextualist approach—not, once again, because it was mine but because I firmly believed that it might do for others what it had done for me and students in my classes.

iii

My first chance to do a critical book came when one of the editors at Twayne Publishers asked me if I would like to do a volume or two in their English Novelists Series. Although Dickens, my first choice, had already been assigned, Charlotte and Emily Bronte, my next two choices, were still available; and since I had a genuine interest in both writers I signed a contract on the spot—never realizing until much later, when I got around to looking at some of the other volumes in the series, what a predicament I had got myself into. For the books, though competent and respectable, were little more than introductory texts, written to a formula (imposed by the editors) which limited individual interpretation to a bare minimum. I could, to be sure, offer my own critical interpretations—just as the editor had promised. The catch-22 was that once I had surveyed the other interpretations (a requirement) there was no room for me to develop my own.

I do not mean to blame the editor. In this instance the fault was entirely mine. In my eagerness to overcome the publishing barrier I had agreed to write books that, in the terms set, the terms I had agreed to, I could not possibly write. For a time I tried to convince myself that I might be able to do Emily Bronte, then collaborate with one of my graduate students on the Charlotte volume. But finally I had to give up altogether and let the contracts lapse.

Another publishing project which I undertook on my own at about the same time seemed, in the beginning, to have some chance of success. It was to be a collection of critical essays, all more or less from a contextualist point of view, covering everything from "the writing of fiction" to the criticism of individual novels, and including selections from well-known writers, critics, and aestheticians—selections which, in my judgment, provided the basis for a contextualist approach to the novel. The first publishing house I contacted showed considerable interest in the projected book, perhaps because in my covering letter I stressed its commercial possibilities, pointing out that it might very well be adopted as a supplementary text in courses on the novel. Whereupon one of the editors, a bit more knowledgeable than the rest, wanted to know why he had never heard of contextualism, and since he had never heard of it, why I thought there would be a demand for a book with "contextualist" in the title (I had entitled it *A Contextualist Approach to the Novel*). These questions I found a bit foolish, since I had already dealt with them in my introduction to the book. Nevertheless I reiterated my arguments as diplomatically as I knew how, stressing the fact that many professors and even more students were becoming impatient with the New Criticism, especially as it was being applied to fiction, and might now be willing to consider a radically different approach to the novel.

Whatever the validity of my arguments they were not sufficient to overcome my skeptical editor's doubts, which, he explained, had nothing to do with the book's being different or radical. What worried him were the risks involved in publishing a book labelled contextualist which included so many essays by writers not ordinarily included in such collections, especially when there were a number of other collections of essays, recently published, which included all the familiar names and all the familiar essays. Would it not be possible, he very discreetly asked, for me to omit the word "contextualist" from my title, then include more familiar names and more familiar essays along with a few of the contextualist ones. That way the collection would have a broader appeal and stand a good chance of being successful.

It was, I repeat, a most reasonable offer; I knew it was, even as I felt defeated by it. I couldn't expect the editor to know, or care, about what I was trying to do. From his point of view I was merely trying to get a collection of essays published; and presumably, since I seemed to be a reasonable man, I would be willing to settle for getting a few of my choices included in a more representative collection. No doubt, if I had been a more practical academic, it would also have seemed reasonable to me. After all, I would be getting my name on the book, plus a chance to include a few contextualist essays to which I could then devote a few words in my introduction. In this way I would be getting my foot in the proverbial door, and next time, or the time after that, or some time, the door would come open and I would be able to publish my entire book. Quite possibly, if I had not over the years seen so many academics with their feet in publishing doors, endless doors that never seemed to open, I too might have been prepared to move a foot at a time. Or possibly, if I had not already found so many other doors that I knew I could open, through my teaching, I might have viewed the prospect of editing just another collection of critical essays as tolerable. As it was I found the prospect intolerable: a complete negation of everything I had in mind for the book.

Writing the editor to tell him that I found his suggestions too drastic proved terribly difficult. It was one thing to arrive at my decision in the heat of frustration; quite another to justify such a decision in words that would make sense to the editor. Yet I knew that I must; that if I tried to temporize or compromise I would end up in the same kind of a battle I had been involved in a few years earlier with still another editor. In that instance Angel Flores wrote to ask me if he could include an essay of mine ("Kafka and Octave Mirbeau," *Accent*, Winter, 1957) in an anthology he was putting together on Kafka (*Kafka Today*, 1959). I of course said that he could, at the same time suggesting that I would prefer to substitute a much longer and more fully developed version of the essay. This suggestion met with Flores' complete approval, and all went well until I sent him the new essay, which he promptly sent back with suggested cuts. Then the editorial battle started—a battle that did not end until Flores dropped me completely out of the anthology. It was a dreadfully frustrating experience, and I had no wish to repeat it in trying to whittle my contextualist volume down to a few essays in a representative collection.

Once again I had to confront what were, for me, impossible demands. I could no more bring the kind of critical work I was attempting to do in line with publishers' demands than earlier I could bring my teaching into line with Berkeley's demands. And I could not, carrying the analogy a bit further, expect to find a University of Washington English department among publishers. If I were to continue with my critical writing I would either have to publish it myself or circulate it amongst my friends and students in mimeographed form. Eventually I would find other alternatives, or rather they would be created for me, but at this point I could see no further than the ditto machine.

iv

There are, I realize, inherent dangers in presenting my own conflicts from my own point of view. For no matter how objective I may be in my presentation I am still, of necessity, giving myself the last word. In delineating my defeat at the hands of publishers, for example, it may seem as if, in my anxiety to justify the intensity of my reaction, I have presented myself as an academic version of the Romantic Hero—a contextualist savior who was being prevented from bringing his critical message to the world by a gang of boorish editors who functioned as the unwitting tools of the system. But that is not what I intended; nor, if I have written as well as I should have, what I said—although, in matters so easily misunderstood, an attempt at further clarification may not be amiss.

For someone (in this case "me") to believe that his writings have value is certainly not "Romantic," or even unusual; nor is it Romantic for him to object to having the value of his writings sacrificed to commercial ends. Innumerable writers have done that. But very few—and this of course is what may seem Romantic—have carried their objections to the extremes that I carried mine and then refused to compromise. How, it may be asked, could I presume to set myself up against the wisdom, or, if one wishes, the necessities, that writers had been coping with for centuries? Surely, to do that I had to have some grandiose notion of myself and my writings. To which I can only reply: I had no such notion: I did not see my refusal as any more grandiose than my refusal, as a conscientious objector, to serve in the armed forces. For reasons which I have tried to suggest, but cannot fully explain without attempting a psychoanalytic self-portrait, I could not do as so many other writers had done. I was not refusing to compromise out of a sense of my own virtue but out of a sense of my own limitations. My withdrawal from publishing, consequently, was not a Romantic gesture of defiance but a recognition of my own psychological make-up.

v

While my efforts to publish were going so badly my teaching, and more particularly my graduate teaching, continued to go splendidly. I had, in 1959 or '60 as I recall, developed a graduate course (entitled Theories of Fiction) which involved a close examination of the work of twentieth-century fictional critics in relation to their aesthetic presuppositions. My primary aim in the course, using Stephen Pepper's *The Basis of Criticism in the Arts*, was to get the students to see that there can be no criticism without aesthetic premises or philosophical presuppositions, that the presuppositions, though they may be hidden from both the critic and his readers, are always there, that the critic can no more escape them than he can jump out of his own skin. Then I tried to get the students to analyze the work of various critics in the light of their acknowledged or unacknowledged presuppositions, my ultimate aim being to get them to see that it made little sense to compare, say, Percy Lubbock's criticism of a novel with E. M. Forster's. Their aesthetic premises were so different, their sense of what a novel should be and do so diametrically opposed, that their critical judgments were bound to differ. One was not better than the other; one was different from the other. The most one could ask of any critic was that he be intelligent and consistent in terms of his own aesthetic.

While this approach may seem disarmingly objective, it invariably had, as I knew it would, upsetting consequences. For its ultimate effect was to force the students into a close examination of the nature and implications of their own presuppositions—an examination which proved especially difficult for those students who had been raised, from high school onwards, exclusively on New Criticism. Many of these students, oblivious to the "New" in New Criticism, actually seemed to believe that it came from God, or at least from Plato or Aristotle, that in any case it was synonymous with criticism. Consequently they experienced a considerable shock when they discovered that it was but one of many schools of criticism, a recent academic version of formalism; and their shock became greater still when, as often happened, they came to realize that they themselves had no sense of original sin, no rage for order, or unity, or point-of-view, that the emphases of the New Criticism did not, in fiction at least, express their own sense of what made novels moving as well as meaningful. For some of the other students the shock of recognition was not so great, since many of them had only accepted New Criticism, in so far as they had accepted it, because they had been unaware of any alternatives. And for still others—those who had stubbornly resisted New Criticism without knowing why, and without being able to justify their resistance—there was no shock unless it was the shock of revelation which would enable them to make good their resistance.

Because in those days nearly all the students were in some measure committed to the New Criticism, or in more or less conscious revolt against it, their attempts to explore their own presuppositions created the greatest controversy in the class. But there were a few Marxists who had difficulties too, plus a few impressionists of various descriptions. Then, after Wayne Booth's *Rhetoric of Fiction* appeared in 1961, the adherents of his moralistic criticism had their turn. And I of course had mine. With the help of aestheticians and critics from John Dewey to E. M. Forster to Philip Rahv (especially his "On the Criticism of Fiction," *Kenyon Review*, 1956) I tried to show the meaning and implications (as well as the liabilities) of my own aesthetic presuppositions.

It was, I believe, a great course—or perhaps I should say they were great courses, since they varied so tremendously from year to year. On one occasion the class even made a special request that we meet on a holiday and everyone showed up; on another occasion, a mature graduate student became so incensed at another student's moralistic criticism of *Madame Bovary* that he rose up and hurled a piece of chalk directly at his head. While such explosions were of course unusual, the intensity was nearly always there, and it gave rise to discussions in which the students actually enlarged or developed or showed the fallacies of the works they were discussing. Indeed a number of students later drew upon these discussions in developing the subjects of their theses.

Yet none of the students, I am convinced, gained any more from the course than I did. In trying to demonstrate the validity of my own approach to fiction (given, of course, my contextualist premises) to students still smarting from my comments on their various critical approaches, I found that I had to deal with questions and objections which might never have occurred to me on my own. And because I had to deal with them on the spot, under pressure, in unambiguous terms, I made intellectual leaps that I might otherwise never have made—to discover that I was moving ever closer to the criticism of a novelist whom I had not, till then, taken seriously as a critic.

vi

Why I was so long in discovering my affinity with D. H. Lawrence I do not really know. I had been acquainted with and had tremendous admiration for his fiction since my graduate school days; at one time or another I had taught all of his major novels in my classes—*The Rainbow*, for which I had the greatest admiration, at least a dozen times. His criticism of Hardy's *Jude* and *Tess* I had also known for some time, along with some of his essays in *Phoenix*, which I remember purchasing while I was in Berkeley. Yet somehow I had never responded to Lawrence's critical writing—perhaps because I was put off by his being, as I then saw it, so wildly impressionistic. Or possibly the fascistic implications were too much for me. Or the mystical element. These characteristics I could accept in Lawrence's fiction as annoying but nevertheless essential to his vision. In the criticism, on the other hand, they struck me as being so irrational and looming so large that they overwhelmed everything else he was trying to say.

Then, through working with Lawrence's criticism in the course on Theories of Fiction, I gained a different perspective.

The mystical elements in the criticism I continued to find objectionable. I still do. Yet I came to realize that these elements were neither so crucial nor so overwhelming as I had previously thought; that they were but Lawrence's way of accounting for his insights, and trying to live with them; that in any case the insights themselves went so deep and were so far-reaching that his manner of explaining and justifying them did not seem all that consequential. And the more I read—in *Phoenix, Fantasia of the Unconscious*, and the essays on the novel—the less consequential the mysticism seemed. At some point I even began to doubt whether the mystical elements were, in the last analysis, quite what they had once seemed, whether my negative sensitivity to any trace of mysticism had not caused me to read more into Lawrence's mystical language than was actually there— doubts that, following the publication of the unexpurgated *Lady Chatterley* (1959) tended to become certainties. For in this novel, generally conceded to be Lawrence's final intellectual testament, Lawrence eschews mysticism to show in direct four-letter words "where God is, if He is anywhere." And he shows Him to be, not in some far-off empyrean but in our very guts.

Whether Lawrence was right, or I was right about Lawrence, need not be argued here. The point is that I had found in Lawrence's criticism the ultimate complement to what I myself had been attempting. The primary critical distinctions I had been trying to draw (about everything from the novelist as revolutionary to the genuine and the counterfeit) Lawrence had already drawn, and in terms so direct and uncompromising that they not only provided me with much needed support but also showed me, by precept and example, how I could go much further. Everywhere I turned in Lawrence there were passages which, by their sheer intensity, laid bare the pretensions of our critical verbiage—as in the following paragraphs from his *Introduction to These Paintings*:

> After a fight tooth-and-nail for forty years, [Cézanne] did succeed in knowing an apple, fully; and not quite as fully, a jug or two. That was all he achieved.
> It seems little, and he died embittered. But it is the first step

that counts, and Cézanne's apple is a great deal, more than Plato's Idea. Cézanne's apple rolled the stone from the mouth of the tomb, and if poor Cézanne couldn't unwind himself from his cerements and mental winding-sheet, but had to lie still in the tomb, till he died, still he gave us a chance.

The history of our era is the nauseating and repulsive history of the crucifixion of the procreative body for the glorification of the spirit, the mental consciousness. Plato was an arch-priest of this crucifixion. Art, that handmaid, humbly and honestly served the vile deed, through three thousand years at least. . . .

We, dear reader, you and I, we were born corpses, and we are corpses. I doubt if there is even one of us who has ever known so much as an apple, a whole apple. All we know is shadows, even of apples. Shadows of everything, of the whole world, shadows even of ourselves. We are inside the tomb, and the tomb is wide and shadowy like hell, even if sky-blue by optimistic paint, so we think it is all the world. But our world is a wide tomb full of ghosts, replicas. We are spectres, we have not been able to touch even so much as an apple. Spectres we are to one another. Spectre you are to me, spectre I am to you. Shadow you are even to yourself. And by shadow I mean idea, concept, the abstracted reality, the ego. We are not solid. We don't live in the flesh. Our instincts and intuitions are dead, we live wound round with the winding-sheet of abstraction. And the touch of anything solid hurts us. For our instincts and intuitions, which are our feelers of touch and knowing through touch, they are dead, amputated. We talk and eat and copulate and laugh and evacuate wrapped in our winding-sheets, all the time wrapped in our winding-sheets.

So that Cézanne's apple hurts. It made people shout with pain. And it was not till his followers had turned him again into an abstraction that he was ever accepted. Then the critics stepped forth and abstracted his good apple into Significant Form, and henceforth Cézanne was saved. Saved for democracy. Put safely into the tomb again, and the stone rolled back. The resurrection was postponed once more.

As the resurrection will be postponed *ad infinitum* by the good bourgeois corpses in their cultured winding-sheets. They will run up a chapel to the risen body, even if it is only an apple, and kill it on the spot . . . All is dead, and dead breath preaching with

phosphorescent effulgence about aesthetic ecstasy and Significant Form. If only the dead would bury their dead. But the dead
are not dead for nothing. Who buries his own sort? The dead are
cunning and alert to pounce on any spark of life and bury *it*,
even as they have already buried Cézanne's apple and put up to
it a white tombstone of Significant Form.

Nearly everything Lawrence says in these paragraphs I
had read before in the writings of critics who had preceded
him (notably George Bernard Shaw) and the many who had
come after him—from William Carlos Williams to Alex
Comfort. Yet Lawrence's words still came to me as something of
a revelation: they gave me a new sense of the lengths to which
he himself had gone, and by implication the lengths to which
every critic (as well as every novelist) had to go if he were going
to mark the distinction between apples and Significant Form. It
may seem little, and Lawrence, too, died embittered, but his
apple, like Cézanne's, gave us a chance—and I, for one, was
ready to take it.

vii

As always when I had a new or revised concept that I
wished to introduce into my criticism I thought first of my
classes. How would they respond to Lawrence's apple? Especially when I had already been asking them to look at fiction in relation to Lawrence's phallus and Sancho Panza's belly. Might the
introduction of the apple not seem comical—as if I were merely
adding another item to my contextualist cornucopia? These
questions also reminded me that I had introduced the phallus
and the belly into my version of contextualism without showing
why they had to be there. So it was not just the apples which I
had to account for, but the phallus and the belly as well.

At this point I was thinking only of how I might clarify
matters for my classes. Yet it soon became obvious that if I were
going to undertake a full clarification I would have to do it in

writing—in a critical study of some kind. And that, for a number of reasons, gave me pause. For I knew that what I intended to say would for many academics, including many of my colleagues, be construed as an attack on them that was in the last analysis an attack on literature itself. I also knew—and this I deeply regretted—that I would be taxing the patience of my friends and sympathizers in the department who had for so long been making allowances for my critical deviations. It was one thing for me to introduce flagrant concepts into an otherwise respectable contextualist aesthetic of fiction; quite another for me to insist, in a forthright critical argument, that I had, with the help of Lawrence and numerous other critics, discovered the key to a new understanding of fiction, that this key amounted to nothing less than the recognition of the voice of the phallus and the belly and the apple as the controlling voice of the serious novel.

There were, to be sure, ways in which I could present my new version of contextualism that would make it, if not generally acceptable, at least not quite so outrageous. But the more I considered these devious ways the less inclined I was to follow them. Why, if my aim was to strip the emperor of his clothes, should I make it a strip tease? Why, if my positive aim was to show the inevitable triumph of the real over the ideal in fiction should I resort to literary camouflage? While I had no inclination to flaunt the phallus, or the belly, or the apple, I had even less inclination to present them in literary terms that might, in effect, reduce them to abstractions. To do that would have been tantamount, paraphrasing Lawrence, to burying the risen body in the guise of resurrecting it.

viii

Once I had my own intentions straight, once I realized that I had committed myself to writing directly for the students as straightforwardly as I knew how, with no thought of publication, no concern for possible consequences, the writing itself did not prove as difficult as I had anticipated. I opened with the passage from Lawrence that I quoted above, then drew upon it in discussing Sancho Panza's role in *Don Quixote*— a discussion which provided me with the opening I needed to move from the epigraph I had taken from Flaubert ("Sancho Panza's belly has burst the seams of Venus' girdle") into my own definition of the Panzaic principle:

> Sancho's belly has not only burst the seams of Venus' girdle, it has given the lie to Dulcinea and in fact all of Don Quixote's ideals—much as Lady Chatterley's guts give the lie to Clifford and his ideals in *Lady Chatterley's Lover*:
>
>> "My dear, you speak as if you were ushering it all in! [*i.e.*, 'the life of the human body']. . . . Believe me, whatever God there is is slowly eliminating the guts and alimentary system from the human being, to evolve a higher, more spiritual being."
>>
>> "Why should I believe you, Clifford, when I feel that whatever God there is has at last wakened up in my guts, as you call them, and is rippling so happily there, like Dawn? Why should I believe you, when I feel so very much the contrary?"

In life the rightness of the guts (as against the mind) will depend on one's point of view. In Lawrence's as in all other novels, however, the guts are always right; it is an axiom or principle of the novel that they are always right, that the senses of even a fool can give the lie to even the most profound abstractions of the noblest thinker. And it is this principle I have designated the Panzaic principle, after Sancho Panza.

My next step, after stating the principle in such unqualified terms, was to confront those critics who had either denied the principle outright or imposed qualifications which rendered it truistic or inconsequential. And since, in my opinion, no one had done a more thorough job of qualifying than Ian Watt, in his chapter on *Tom Jones* (*The Rise of the Novel*, 1957) I began with that—tracing all Watt's squirmings and turnings as he uses everything from literary history to "larger moral significance" to convince himself and his readers that what takes place in the novel either does not mean what it clearly seems to mean or, if it does mean that, its meaning does not matter because it lacks Watt's "larger moral significance." When Tom Jones goes into the bushes with Molly Seagrim he is, according to Watt, "no more than a vehicle for the expression of Fielding's scepticism about lovers' vows" whose function is to illustrate the desexualized commonplace that "actions speak louder than words." The relation of this episode to "the larger structure of the novel," Watt explains, is therefore typical:

> The relation of this episode to the larger structure of the novel is typical. One of Fielding's general organising themes is the proper place of sex in human life; this encounter neatly illustrates the conflicting tendencies of headstrong youth, and shows that Tom has not yet reached the continence of moral adulthood. The scene, therefore, plays its part in the general moral and intellectual scheme; and it is also significantly connected with the workings of the plot, since Tom's lapse eventually becomes a factor in his dismissal by Allworthy, and therefore leads to the ordeals which eventually make him a worthier mate for Sophia.

In showing how neatly Watt structured the Panzaic not only out of this episode but out of the entire novel I had not, except perhaps by implication, done much to indicate what my own reading of Tom Jones would be. But that was not my intention. In this, as in my further critiques of E.M.W. Tillyard, George Orwell, Cleanth Brooks, Robert B. Heilman, Americo Castro, and Dorothy van Ghent I had but one aim: to analyze the various ways in which these various critics had tried to acknowledge the force of the Panzaic—only to stop short when that force threatened their various conceptions of art and culture and civilization.

But there was one critic who did not stop short, who had the courage to face up to "the force of the concrete in things." I am speaking of Ortega y Gasset, and it was to him that I turned in my final attempt to clarify the Panzaic:

> The force of the concrete in things stops the movement of our images. The inert and harsh object rejects whatever "meanings" we may give it: it is just there, confronting us, affirming its mute, terrible materiality in the face of all phantoms. This is what we call realism: to bring things to a distance, place them under a light, incline them in such a way that the stress falls upon the side which slopes down towards pure materiality . . . The theme of realistic poetry is the crumbling of poetry . . . the poetic quality of reality is not reality as this or that thing but reality as a generic function. Therefore it does not actually matter what objects the realist chooses to describe. Any one at all will do, since they all have an imaginary halo around them . . . Materiality [provides] a conclusive argument, a critical power which defeats the claim to self-sufficiency of all idealizations, wishes and fancies of man. The insufficiency, in a word, of culture, of all that is noble, clear, lofty . . . Cervantes recognizes that culture is all that, but that, alas, it is a fiction. Surrounding culture—as the puppet show of fancy was surrounded by the inn—lies the barbarous, brutal, mute, insignificant reality of things. It is sad that it is shown to us thus, but what can we do about it! It is real, it is there: it is terribly self-sufficient. Its force and its single meaning are rooted in its presence. Culture is memories and promises, an irreversible past, a dreamed future. But reality is a simple and frightening "being there." It is a presence, a deposit, an inertia. It is materiality.

Here, at long last, I had a critic diametrically opposed to my own critical position (and to Lawrence's) whose every word tended to validate the distinctions I had been trying to draw between the ideal and the real, culture and materiality—finally to show, in words more eloquent than mine, that the apple, the belly, and the phallus possess a power which "defeats the claim to self-sufficiency of all idealizations, wishes and fancies of man . . . The insufficiency, in a word, of culture, of all that is noble, clear, lofty . . ."

More significant still, for my purposes, Ortega demonstrated how this power, the power of the Panzaic, had become
basic to the novel as an art form, how in every novel it destroys
the myth, "the crystalline orb of the ideal":

> The novel of adventures, the tale, the epic are that ingenuous
> manner of experiencing imaginary and significant things. The
> realistic novel is this second oblique manner. It requires some-
> thing of the first: it needs something of the mirage to make us see
> it as such. So that it is not only *Don Quixote* which was written
> against the books of chivalry, and as a result bears the latter
> within it, but the novel as a literary genre consists essentially of
> that absorption.
>
> This offers an explanation of . . . how reality, the actual, can
> be changed into poetic substance. By itself, seen in a direct way,
> it would never be poetic: this is the privilege of the mythical. But
> we can consider it obliquely as destruction of the myth, as criti-
> cism of the myth. In this form reality, which is of an inert and
> insignificant nature, quiet and mute, acquires movement, is
> changed into an active power of aggression against the crystal-
> line orb of the ideal. The enchantment of the latter broken, it
> falls into fine, iridescent dust which gradually loses its colours
> until it becomes an earthy brown. We are present at this scene in
> every novel. There is need of a book showing in detail that every
> novel bears the *Don Quixote* within it like an inner filigree in the
> same way that every epic poem contains the Iliad within it like
> the fruit its core.

Ortega's "every novel," I went on to explain, obviously did
not include the thousands of best-selling and counterfeit novels
that exclude Panzaic reality altogether. Nor did it seem to
include those few novels that E. M. Forster had defined as
"prophetic." Yet Forster's exceptions, I argued, did not invali-
date Ortega's analysis. At worst they merely qualified it. "Every
novel" may not bear the *Don Quixote* within it, but nearly all
the serious ones do. The voice of reality is always "there"—in a
way and to a degree and with effects that bear out Ortega's fears
and Lawrence's hopes.

ix

This first version of "The Panzaic Principle," I soon came to realize, left far too much room for critical misunderstandings. Yet even with its shortcomings it did just about everything I had hoped it would. In my undergraduate classes I distributed mimeographed copies the first week of each quarter and then invited the students to have a direct go at it and me—in the hope that the discussion would clarify the issues that were always lurking beneath the surface of docility that every new class seemed to assume. And more often than not the Panzaic principle did its work—in part, no doubt, because the students found the discussion of apples and bellies and phalluses a bit more exciting than the discussions of form and technique to which they were accustomed. There was, however, more to it than that, or at any rate more could be made out of it. One student, for example, observed that he had always thought that his responses to fiction were just his "dirty mind;" now he felt much better because he could see that they conformed to the Panzaic principle. A naive remark, to be sure, yet I could still answer, in all seriousness, that he was essentially correct, that as readers they had to develop dirty minds in order to understand what goes on in novels. They had to do this, I insisted, in order to free themselves from a delusion common amongst students: that serious fiction, particularly serious fiction of the past, is as innocent, as moralistically idyllic, as George Eliot's *Silas Marner*, when, in point of fact, it is more like *Jane Eyre*, or George Eliot's own *Daniel Deronda*, and invariably contains passages, often crucial passages, which can only be understood by readers with "dirty minds."

At the same time I had to caution the students that the "dirt" had to be there, textually there; that the Panzaic principle was not a new kind of hunting license which would justify their reading-in dirt that exists nowhere but in their own minds. At this point another student might bring up the old saying, "If you're looking for dirt you'll always find it." Which would give me the chance to point out that the saying might very well be applicable to life in general, but not to the serious novel, which (in contrast to the popular novel) seldom gives the reader what he is looking for. In this connection I might also remind the students that E. M. Forster's test for a "round" character (a treacherous test, but all right as a rule of thumb) is the character's ability to "surprise convincingly."

Whereupon another student, a bright but surly male who had been irritated by the whole discussion, might bring me and the class back to our original subject with a series of accusations cast in the form of questions: "But what's the point of finding the 'dirt,' even if it's there? Who cares if Don Quixote shits? Maybe, since Lawrence brings up water-closets, the Panzaic principle should be called the water-closet theory of fiction." Answering the last question first I would have to acknowledge that I would be willing to stand by Lawrence's statement ("In the novel, in contrast to poems and plays, there's always a tom-cat, a black tom-cat that pounces on the white dove of the Word . . . and there is a banana skin to trip on; and you know there is a water-closet on the premises.") and I would also be obliged to acknowledge that the Panzaic theory of fiction might very well be called "the water-closet theory"—although I preferred to call it the Panzaic principle. And I would likewise have to agree that the mere fact of Don Quixote's shitting is not, in itself, of any great interest. What is interesting in the novel is when he shits, and why, for the when and the why go a long way towards reducing "the crystalline orb" in the novel to "an earthy brown."

"But who," someone might question, "wants to see ideals, and more especially his own ideals, reduced to shit? Even if they are shit who wants to know it? How do we then live if we do know it?" After these ultimate questions there was always a long pause, as if the students (as a class) recognized that we had arrived at the point of no return in our discussion. And they were of course right. From this point onwards, I explained, I could no longer presume to give answers. I could only give my answers and suggest possible alternatives—the alternatives which were, with one exception, already implicit or explicit in the critical works I had surveyed in "The Panzaic Principle." The final decision had to be theirs, for it was no longer a literary decision but a personal one—on which their sense of themselves and their conception of the world they lived in might well depend.

By this time a number of students would have become terribly "bored," their way of avoiding anything in literature or in discussion that threatened their composure. But that was all right, since I no longer had to worry about their reactions. They could take care of themselves. Others would be genuinely puzzled—as if the classroom were turning into a church. And that was all right too, since their puzzlement might lead to understanding. A few others might be genuinely interested, which was of course what I was hoping for. And still others might be genuinely upset to find themselves being drawn into a discussion which seemed to be playing upon their deepest feelings. One such student, upon reaching the end of his patience, stood up in class, all the while pointing his finger at me, to declare: "You're a great big phony." To which I could only reply, since his announcement came at the very end of the class, "No, I'm not, and I'll explain why I'm not tomorrow."

The great thing about such challenges was the way in which they broke the tension, cleared the atmosphere. Many other students also saw me as a phony, or at the very least suspected me of being one. Of that I was certain, on the basis of my experiences with previous classes. The problem always was how to get these feelings and suspicions out into the open, and the student's challenge had done that, giving me the opportunity, the next day, to confess that I might have given the appearance of being pietistic or pretentious in the way I was presenting the choices they were confronted with, that it was difficult for me not to give this appearance, since I looked upon their choices as being very close to a life and death matter. But whatever appearances I gave I was not, I assured them, being a phony. The way I presented their choices and everything connected with them was the way I myself understood the choices. Yet how they viewed me, I went on to explain, should not be the final test. The presentation I was making would be equally valid, intellectually if not emotionally, whether I were sincere or not—provided it was intelligent and consistent.

Then, getting back to their choices, I could say in all sincerity that many of them might very well decide to give up the reading of serious novels altogether—on the ground that they were, measured against their own ideals, not only "dirty" but completely immoral. There were, I explained, innumerable versions of this choice—from Archibald MacLeish to Van Wyck Brooks to various authoritarian versions which could be traced all the way back to Plato, who would have limited poets to the writing of patriotic songs. Yet however defensible any of these versions might be in its own terms I did not, I had to tell the students, see how it could be made compatible with what we were attempting in class. If, for example, they were devout Christians, they might come to see me and many others in the class as their tormentors, and I, for one, had no wish to assume such a role. Usually, however, my words of warning had little effect. If a few students dropped, more stayed to be tormented—perhaps because they wanted to see if it would really happen, or perhaps because they really wanted it to happen. And many times I was glad they did stay, especially when, as was often the case, they gave a good account of themselves in class discussion and on their papers and exams.

For those students who did not hold their ideals as something sacred or unassailable, who were, on the positive side, determined to hang onto both their ideals and serious fiction there were, I suggested, the many critical alternatives I had recapitulated in "The Panzaic Principle," ranging all the way from Ian Watt's invocation of "greater moral significance" to Dorothy van Ghent's inversion of the Panzaic in her "insight made body." In the work of one or more of these critics, I explained, they would in all likelihood find the answers they were looking for. And I, on my side, would do my best to respect their answers—even as I questioned them and tried to point out their implications.

Or they could, if they were willing to develop dirty minds, and say "to hell with culture" whenever the novels seemed to be saying it, choose the Panzaic. That, I repeated, would be my own approach. And while I would never, I promised, try to impose it on them *ex cathedra*, I would do everything in my power to give it full expression—in the hope that it might do for some of them what I thought it had done for me. Or, a lesser hope, that exposure to the Panzaic would at least enlarge their "larger moral significance," and broaden their conception of form and technique.

Much of what I have included in this reconstruction of what took place in the opening sessions of my undergraduate classes I had said before. But never with so much directness. The Panzaic principle had not only helped me to discover the controlling voice of serious fiction, it had freed me from the psychological constraints I had been laboring under in my classes. If Lawrence and Ortega could say what they were saying in print, surely I could say as much in my classes—so long as I said it, not to bait or beat or titillate the students, but to bring them to an understanding of fiction that would not end in "appreciation" but would, hopefully, bring them to a better understanding of their own selves, including their Panzaic selves, and their own world, including the real as well as the ideal in that world.

That was what I was attempting in my undergraduate classes, and that, I believe, is what I achieved during these years. Not in terms of numbers. I had never been, except perhaps in my earliest years of teaching at Miami and Cornell and Harvard, a popular teacher. Students had never flocked to my classes. And the Panzaic principle and what I was doing with it, made my courses even less attractive to most students—to a point where I might have had difficulty in filling my classes if I had not become known as a fairly easy grader. But what I was interested in, or it might be more accurate to say "dedicated to," had nothing to do with popularity or numbers. If three or four or five students out of some twenty could gain an adequate understanding of what I was attempting in a class, that class was, for me, a successful one. And I had more successes after I introduced the Panzaic than ever before.

X

It was in my graduate classes, however, that the Panzaic principle had the deepest and most far-reaching effects. Because the graduate students were, in comparison with the under-graduates, so much more knowledgeable and sophisticated in critical matters they could see almost immediately that the Panzaic had virtually unlimited possibilities; that it could, if carried to its logical conclusions, make a shambles of the then dominant schools of fictional criticism; that it could do to them what Sancho had done to the good Don and his books of chivalry, what Falstaff had done to Henry IV and his ideals of kingship. To some few graduate students, including of course those who were already sympathetic to my point of view, these possibilities seemed exciting, or even exhilarating; to others who were somewhat sympathetic but inclined to be more cynical, they seemed futile; and to still others they seemed downright heretical—a threat to everything they believed in. "How," one of these students asked rather plaintively, "can you, a cultured man, even suggest that we give up Art and Culture? Art and Culture have made you what you are. And besides, how can you suggest that we throw away all our knowledge of myths and symbols, all our critical skills and techniques—after we have spent years acquiring them?"

My answer to these questions probably went on for hours, with various students having their say along with mine. But in essence what I said was that I recognized the difficulties the student had raised; that perhaps, if I had come along twenty years later, and been brought up on the criticism he had been brought up on, I too might feel that I was throwing away my cultural heritage as well as my years of critical labor. But luckily, owing to my growing up when and how I did, I had escaped all that, and now I could help him and others to escape it too. For surely, once he realized that his myths and symbols were Don Quixote's "crystalline orb," he would not wish to hang onto them. How could he when they were denying his own guts, his own phallus? Did he want to sacrifice them along with Cézanne's apple, to abstract concepts of Art and Culture, with all the life-denying imperatives, all the demands for order and obedience, that they invariably imposed?

Then, moderating my tone a bit, I would point out to the students that the Panzaic principle did not ask them to give up their knowledge and their skills. Readers and critics need to know about the "crystalline orb," in all its manifestations, so that they can better understand what is happening in the novel when "the force of the concrete in things" smashes it to bits. A novelist friend of mine from Montana once remarked that he wished all readers could read the way a sheepherder reads; then, after a moment of thought, he went on to add: "if a sheepherder knew how to read a novel." And that, with a reverse twist, is what the Panzaic principle is asking of us: that we become sheepherders who can, because of the knowledge and skills we have already acquired, read novels.

At this point someone would invariably raise the question: "But what about standards? Who is to say what is good and bad?" And that would send me and the class into more hours of discussion which, on my side, went something like this: standards are mostly silly: good taste, as Emerson, I think, said, is but a poor substitute for individual perception; or, as Flaubert said, good taste is deadly; give me someone with bad taste and there may be some hope for him. And by now, good taste has become an industry, in literature as well as in the other arts, in the little magazines as well as in *Harpers* or *PMLA*. In fiction its tests are complexity, unity, organic form, etc; tests which as often as not certify novels as good or even great which have nothing but fashionable appeals to "archetypal myth" and technical dexterity to recommend them. As novels they are as "dead," as counterfeit, as those which Queenie Leavis dealt with in her *Fiction and The Reading Public* (1939). So what standards do we have to lose—except those which seek to elevate the dead and the counterfeit to a semblance of life.

What the Panzaic principle provides, I would go on to point out, is a chance, on the positive side, to start all over: to read the novels in the way Lawrence and Ortega suggest; more specifically, following Ortega's suggestion, to see if they really do contain the *Don Quixote* within them, if they really do smash the "crystalline orb"—in what ways, to what end. And then, by way of standards, if we must have them, to see which novels give us the fullest deepest sense of "life" through the characters and their interactions with each other and "the concrete in things;" that is, the fullest deepest sense of what we are like in our guts and in our phalluses—as well as in our minds—in relation to the world as it exists in apples as well as in the abstractions which deny us and the apples.

Although I have presented what I myself said almost exclusively, the classes were not monologues. The points I have covered in summary fashion would have involved hours of discussion, usually heated discussion, and they would have turned on specific aspects of specific novels as well as on theoretical considerations. Not very many students could accept the Panzaic as I presented it but the few who did often went beyond me in their youthful enthusiasm.

One of these students, Arthur Efron, now a professor at SUNY (Buffalo), had been working on his thesis with me when I wrote "The Panzaic Principle;" and when he went to Buffalo in 1963, he devised a kind of little magazine called *Paunch*. In the beginning it was not much more than a mimeographed newsletter, made up of comments and informal papers through which he and his friends from Washington (many of whom had already found positions in other universities) shared their views on life and literature. For Efron, as for everyone else involved, *Paunch* filled a very real need, and in less than a year he began developing it into a full-fledged journal.

Although I had contributed nothing more to *Paunch* than moral support, I was, needless to say, much pleased with the way it developed, and still more pleased when Efron asked me if I would like to publish "The Panzaic Principle" in *Paunch* number 22, along with any graduate papers on the Panzaic which I considered interesting. And when number 22 appeared (January, 1965), in an adequate format, with Daniel Callahan's telling version of Sancho on the front cover, and with two excellent papers accompanying "The Panzaic Principle" (Wendy Bowman Morris' "Panzaism and Dostoevsky" and Caroline Brigham's "The Panzaic Principle in *Villette*") I felt proud indeed that we had accomplished so much. At the same time, however, I had few if any illusions about the future. I did not see this issue of *Paunch* as heralding the beginnings of a new critical movement that would eventually gain general acceptance. My experience in my classes had convinced me that the Panzaic could appeal to only a few stray individuals, and I was content with that. I had no wish to see *Paunch* become a Panzaic *Kenyon Review*. I thought it was already doing everything it could do—that the measure of its achievement would be its ability to continue doing just what it had been doing.

That too was the way I looked upon my own teaching and advising and writing. I thought I was finally accomplishing what I had been trying to accomplish, and I wanted only time to do more.

xi

My only serious conflicts during these years were with the department, over the Ph.D. theses I was supervising. I continued to have more than my share of really outstanding students, and that fact, coupled with what I was encouraging them to do in their theses, severely strained my relations with several members of the department, finally erupting in direct conflict over Michael Steig's brilliant thesis on Dickens. There is no need to rehash the details here—except to note that, in the end, Steig had no choice but to rewrite parts of his thesis to the specifications of the objecting professor, and I, unless I were going to fight it out with no regard for Steig's predicament, had no choice but to approve the revisions. It was a bitter blow, made all the more bitter for me because I had to give in, without a fight, to objections which I considered puerile.

How much of this conflict stemmed from the Panzaic principle I could not be certain. Steig had made no direct references to the Panzaic, nor was it mentioned directly in the ensuing controversy. But I remained apprehensive. Not to take chances I henceforth advised students to avoid direct references to the Panzaic in their theses, telling them that they could still employ the concepts without the identifying name. Yet there were still difficulties. In the case of David Smith's thesis, originally entitled *Incest in Five Victorian Novels*, a friend of mine in the department jokingly suggested that it might be called *Familial Relations in Five Victorian Novels*, and we ultimately settled on *The Arrested Heart: Interfamilial Love in Five Mid-Victorian Novels*.

In themselves incidents of this kind were not too consequential; indeed they often had their amusing side. And much of the kidding I took about the Panzaic that sounded a bit harsh I knew to be entirely good-natured—as, for instance, when Theodore Roethke introduced me to a distinguished visiting poet as "the armpit of the department." But there were other instances which had a grimmer aspect; for example, students telling me, in terms which left no doubt about their veracity, that they had been advised by other members of the department not to work with me on their theses; that if they did so they would be lessening their chances of getting through and getting a job. As a matter of fact I myself always mentioned these liabilities to students when they discussed the possibility of my becoming their supervisor; but a colleague's doing the job for me carried with it the ugly suggestion that he and the department would make the student suffer if he still chose me.

The open disagreements I did not mind, and I had to hope that my colleagues did not mind either. Heilman, I knew, did not object to my taking issue with him (in "The Panzaic Principle" itself) over his and Brooks' treatment of Falstaff in their *Introduction to Drama*. Although he and I had argued the same issues many times before, I showed him a typescript of what I planned to say before I included it in the essay—in an effort to make sure he did not find it offensive. And I tried, for the most part successfully, I think, to keep my open disagreements with other members of the department from becoming personal—no mean feat when everything I was writing, everything I was saying, pushed me further and further outside the pale of academic criticism.

Then too, beginning in 1963, there were the essays and comments of graduate students or former graduate students appearing in *Paunch*. Because Efron made a point of sending copies of *Paunch* to various members of the department at Washington, in an effort to get them to respond, the essays and comments created quite a stir around Parrington Hall. And when *Paunch* number 21 appeared, with a long and somewhat pugnacious essay by Efron himself entitled "Why Christian Can't Read," one member of the department, David Fowler, felt obliged to express his doubts about *Paunch* in what were, for him, rather severe terms (*Paunch, #22*, p. 75):

> I have read *Paunch* #21 through and found it fascinating if not entirely satisfying. I keep hoping I can find the fallacy in my belief that everyone in your group faces the dilemma of Baudelaire . . . (& his successors) needing bourgeois morality to condemn him. If your position is not actually *parasitic*, then what is your position? Do you make a distinction between man and the animals? If so, what is the distinction? Or if these questions seem unfair in that they demand a metaphysic, in what other way can you make your own world-view clear? Thus far I seem unable to infer it from your criticisms of other positions.

Fowler's were honest doubts, and Efron wrote an intelligent reply—although it was not quite the reply I myself would have written. In my classes I had for years been using the word "parasitic," not apologetically or defensively but descriptively, to identify my own particular brand of anarchism, my aim being to meet head-on the objections which I knew were coming, usually in the form of questions. What if everyone became an anarchist? What would happen to the sewer system? etc., etc. These questions, I knew, expressed genuine fears, and I had no wish to treat them lightly; but they would also, if I tried to answer them in their own terms, lock me into the questioner's own political thinking—from which there could be no escape short of the answers I had to give: that there was no danger whatsoever that any but a very few individuals were ever going to become anarchists of my sort; that consequently there was no need to worry about an alternative political system, or about the sewer system either. In my kind of anarchism there was no thought of overturning the political structure, or establishing another one. To try to do that was to get involved in organizations, and organizations, even the most liberal organizations, were deadly in the sense that the individual had to sacrifice his individuality to them. For an anarchist the most corrupt governments were often, as my friend George Woodcock had long ago argued, the best, since they had no interest in getting everybody into line. As parasitic anarchists our test of a social-political system, corrupt or not, was how much room it left for the individual to escape, or, in E. M. Forster's words, how many "breathing-holes" it left open for those who had no wish to join up or fit in.

Although I never at any time went around Parrington Hall proclaiming these ideas, which were, needless to say, of a piece with my Panzaic ones, nearly all my colleagues had by this time become aware that my views were strangely heretical. Worse still, they were coming to recognize that I would not in all likelihood change—except perhaps for the worse. After all, I was in my forties, and showing no signs of development—except in the wrong directions. As the department was organizing itself more and more tightly into a smooth-running, high-powered, run-of-the-mill, first-rate department, with less and less room for deviation, I was not only becoming more and more deviant but also taking a good number of graduate students with me.

What saved me, I believe, was the fact that Heilman and many of the other senior members of the department had so much of their old tolerance, their old openness, their old integrity still left in them. Fowler's letter, for example, in which he expressed his doubts about *Paunch*, could hardly have been more fair—and yet Efron's essay, "Why Christian Can't Read," although it did not mention Fowler by name, applied directly to his criticism as well as his teaching. Whether, by this time, the department would have hired me, and given me tenure, and promoted me, if I had just been appearing on the scene, I am not at all sure. But they were stuck with me, and willing to put up with me, and that was all I could reasonably ask. I never for a moment expected them to cherish me in my deviations.

In thus viewing my situation in the department with so much equanimity I was not in any sense being heroic, or even stoical. I had a few good friends who were also colleagues who continued to cherish me; I had numerous graduate students and former graduate students who were not only good friends but willing to go all the way with me in my deviant explorations; I had been having more success in both my graduate and undergraduate classes than ever before; I had, through *Paunch*, found ways around my difficulties with publishers; I had, in short, arrived at where I had been trying to go—and it was all so good, so satisfying, that my highest ambition was to be able to keep on going.

7

As the Walls
Come Tumbling Down
(1965–1972)

THE CHANGES which the world, including the academic world, went through in the late sixties and early seventies might seem to be changes which I should have welcomed. That they were not, that they turned my world into something of a nightmare, therefore requires some explanation, beginning with the reasons why I found nearly all the causes and movements of the time, causes and movements which I had hitherto believed in and supported, in so far as a parasitic anarchist could, so entirely unacceptable.

I had no sympathy with the Vietnam war. As a life long pacifist how could I? Yet I could not help viewing the students' anti-war protests as naive or misguided or inadequate. How could they be conscientious objectors to this particular war? That was simply an acknowledgement that if there were another Pearl Harbor they would be willing and ready to enlist. I could see, of course, that even limited objection might serve an immediate useful purpose if it enabled those making the objections to escape serving—just as I could see that any other tactic, from running to Canada to faking illnesses or disabilities, might serve an immediate useful purpose. For that matter I could even see faking patriotism, after the manner of Schweik in *The Good Soldier Schweik*. But the students in the anti-war protests never, as a group, seemed to be faking. A few individuals in the group were, I knew, but they had little effect on the movement, which seemed to me bogus as well as ineffectual. By equating war resistance with patriotic resistance to an unjust war it made all-out resistance to war that much more difficult in this country—as evidenced by the fact that even now, when there is no immediate threat from Russia, the only people saying "better Red than dead" are in Europe.

In characterizing the anti-Vietnam movement in this way, I am, I realize, laying myself open to all sorts of objections. It can be argued that I am the one who was naive, that by making their protests limited and patriotic the students worked within our political system to accomplish what no other protesters had ever accomplished—by hastening the end of the war. And that, it can also be argued, could never have been accomplished by the sort of anti-war resistance I was advocating. But this final argument, it seems to me, once again means surrender to the system—in this case the war-making elements of our system—in that it limits protest to what the system will accept, and if the system finds that a Vietnam war arouses too much resistance it will see to it that the next war, whether it be another Vietnam or not, will be much better orchestrated.

ii

Some of the other movements I felt less strongly about. Racial issues had never touched me personally as I was growing up: there was only one black in Winchester; one Jew and several blacks in Georgetown, none of whom I knew or came in contact with. At Miami and Harvard I became increasingly aware of racial inequalities, but not so much through experience as through association with radical groups and through my own reading in liberal and radical journals. It was not until I went to Duke, and lived in Durham, North Carolina, that I had any direct sense of racial discrimination, and I found it at once sickening and incomprehensible. But for whatever reasons I did not respond as some of my friends did, perhaps because there had been nothing in my background to give me a sense of racial guilt. Racism was terribly inhuman, but so were many other things in our society, and I could not, right up to the late sixties, see how they could be righted through social or political action.

Once again my point is not to vindicate my feelings or my anarchist ideas but to describe them—to show how I could fail to respond to the arguments and appeals and pressures that the black movement began to exert on university campuses. When, at the height of the furor, the English department gathered in solemn conclave, to be told by a visiting black, a young graduate student from somewhere, how and what we should teach in our classes, in so far as our teaching related to blacks, I could hardly believe what I was seeing and hearing. One professor, a crusty conservative, did manage to ask if "they had a black physics yet," but the graduate student was more than equal to that when he answered: "No, we don't, but we're working on it, and we'll let you know when we do." At this point, since I was still having difficulty in believing that it could all be serious, I started to laugh a bit—at what I thought was the graduate student's clever way of pretending to talk like a gauleiter. Yet as far as I could tell no one else laughed, and the graduate student never cracked a smile.

Perhaps, in recounting this episode I have been unfair. There were, I know, others in the department who reacted to the graduate student's directives in essentially the same way I did. But they then proceeded to make allowances or excuses which in effect amounted to saying that black fascism could not be fascism, and anyhow there was no harm in listening to the directives since they could never be enforced without black storm troopers.

I knew better, as I shall explain presently when I discuss my classroom experiences. And I soon learned, when I gave a talk on literature and anarchism at Seattle Community College, that the storm troopers were there too. I had just begun speaking when a young black woman entered the room quite flamboyantly with two black males—as if they had dropped in to check up on the proceedings. Which, as the question period soon revealed, was exactly what they were doing. The woman immediately took on the role of inquisitor, wanting to know why I had made no mention of blacks or the black movement, and demanding that I make an effort to redeem myself. It was a ticklish situation in that I was tempted to tell her that I had never answered such demands and could see no reason why I should answer hers. But I restrained myself long enough to explain that I saw no hope in organized movements, black or any other kind; that I did not see blacks as special people but people; that I could like and perhaps, if I had the chance, love a black person but not a black organization. By the time I had finished I myself was in a good humor and the woman too seemed at least partially satisfied. She commented that she could see no great harm in what I was saying, that it sounded like misguided Christianity, and since Les McIntosh (now a black leader in the movement who had once been a student of mine) had vouched for my good intentions, I might be permitted to continue. At which point she got up and strode out of the room with the two black males (Black Panthers, I have since been told) trailing along behind her. And the people who remained, having, understandably, no further questions, soon began to make their way out with as much dignity as they could muster.

My point is not that this was a dreadful experience for me. On the contrary. Once I accepted the fact that I was being grilled I rather enjoyed having my say. Moreover I rather liked the woman, just as I had rather liked the dictatorial graduate student, and just as I had really liked Les McIntosh, wild man that he was. But what I liked was their courage, not their actions, not their browbeating. Fascistic tactics were no better when they were practiced by organized blacks than when they were practiced by organized whites.

iii

The feminist movement, in its earliest manifestations, seemed more like a flurry than a movement, and for some time, I failed to take it very seriously. Not because I had any feelings against women, or against their announced objectives, but because I could not see why they had to organize themselves separately, as women, in order to achieve those objectives. Why, if they had to have organizations, did they have to be women's organizations? Surely they could work through the man-woman organizations already in existence, or if need be organize new and hopefully better ones, and thus avoid exacerbating the male-female split that Lawrence, in his novels, had shown to be so destructive.

As the flurry became a movement, however, it began to take on all the characteristics of the black movement, which it was in large measure, whether consciously or not, modelled after. Lawrence was lambasted; Freud became anathema; the clitoris assumed larger sexual as well as moral significance; and feminist women began to assume the very organizational attitudes which they found so offensive in men—attitudes which I, for my part, found as offensive in women as I had found them in men.

iv

The ecological movement, it has been said, was cooked up by high-level bureaucrats as a means of siphoning off young people's energies from social-political protest into more positive and more easily controlled channels: bicycles instead of bombs, clean air instead of black power, environment instead of revolution. But if the movement was cooked up the ingredients for it were already there; in fact they had been there since as early as 1957, when Kerouac, in his *Dharma Bums*, presented a fictional recipe for the entire ecological movement. I can no longer recall whether the bicycles are in the novel but nearly everything else is, from the rucksacks to the mountain climbing to the cooking to the spiritual qualities appropriate to these activities. Kerouac's Japhy Ryder, moreover, is a true American hero (modelled after Gary Snyder): "What hope, what energy, what truly American optimism was packed in that neat little frame of his." And in the final pages of the novel Kerouac's narrator waxes poetic—to foresee thousands of Japhys, their packs on their backs, hiking joyfully through the suburbs on the way to freedom and fulfillment on the mountain top, in the form of salami and Ry-Krisp and Dharma.

These Ry-Krisp sentimentalities I never could abide, even when, in the late fifties, I was trying to defend the Beats; and I found the hippie version of the early sixties and the ecological versions of the late sixties even less excusable—in part I suppose, because they turned my own version of parasitic anarchism, which actually did, as I saw it, promise a realistic hope of individual fulfillment, into something groupy and sentimental. And when the ecological version began to develop into a movement, with many of the characteristics of the black and feminist movements, I could no more tolerate their pieties than I could their demands, particularly when their demands were couched in language that revealed the police mentality behind them. Since I had never thought of wasting energy, or killing whales, or littering, the demand that I nevertheless feel guilty and desist, in the name of the environment and good citizenship, struck me as gratuitous bullying. Nor was I much impressed by the argument that the bullying was in a good cause, and therefore inevitably for my own good. That argument had been used by authoritarians of every description from the beginning of history.

v

Neither drugs nor mysticism, as I encountered them, could be called movements: they were rather prime ingredients in the outward forms of escapism and rebellion which began to manifest themselves in the middle and late fifties, primarily in the activities and writings of the Beats and hippies. My direct experiences with drugs, beginning with marijuana when I was at Pasadena in 1955, were rather limited and invariably disappointing—in large measure, perhaps, because I found the idea of such forms of stimulation or escape philosophically if not morally repugnant. As long as young people had their five senses, and some chance to use and develop them, I could not see why they wanted to opt for kicks or nirvana, which, as I saw them, would inevitably be lesser states of being. For the old or the sick or the totally lost drugs might be the answer, but not for the young and healthy.

At the time these arguments sounded terribly stuffy, even moralistic, especially coming from someone who identified himself as a Panzaic and parasitic anarchist. And my objections to Zen and all the other current forms of mysticism sounded equally contradictory. Yet I could not see that there were any contradictions whatsoever. Drugs and mysticism were ultimately denials of the body as well as the mind. They were the new opiates of the new young people.

Once again I must emphasize that I am not trying to justify my intellectual outlook on these matters. I am merely trying to indicate, in general terms, what it was. Always before I had been more or less in sympathy with, more or less lined up with, the liberal and radical movements of my day. Now, for the first time, I found myself opposed to just about everything young people considered liberal or radical. I was, in short, in something like the same position as that described by another anarchist, Paul Goodman, in his *New Reformation: Notes of a Neolithic Conservative*, the big difference being that my brand of anarchism also cut me off from his neolithic alternative.

vi

The "sexual revolution," which might, as I observed it at the University of Washington, be more accurately labelled the "sexual movement," accompanied the social-political movements of the late sixties, and in many respects derived from them. When I first taught the unexpurgated *Lady Chatterley* in 1959 many of the women in my undergraduate class were shocked by the four-letter words. While they knew what the words meant, they had never encountered them in print or in ordinary conversation, much less in class. Ten years later, in a comparable class, many of the women were themselves using four-letter words, and speaking quite freely about everything from clitoral orgasm to incest to lesbianism.

Now superficially, I had to admit, there was nothing wrong with this. The women were merely exercising their freedom and demonstrating their equality. And that, I had to agree, was good: women had to be sexually free as well as socially and politically free or they could not reach the kind of individual fulfillment I had been advocating. What worried me, however, was what had worried Lawrence forty years earlier, when he pointed out the dangers inherent in translating human impulses into abstractions, and, in matters of sex, getting the sex into the head, not down where it belongs. For once sex gets into the head, Lawrence argued, it turns the human body into a machine for pleasure or a machine for power.

But that, it may be objected, is mere poetry, and not very good poetry at that. Sex is always in the head, and always has been. Or at least it has always been in men's heads, and therefore why not women's. To deny women this freedom is a disguised put-down of women. Besides the women were not just talking sex; many of them were acting out their words and concepts. They had begun acting them out in the hippie pads and communes, and by the late sixties they were acting them out wherever they chose. And their acting-out, it seemed to me, had taken on the characteristics that Lawrence predicted. The fault, if it was a fault, was not entirely theirs. They were, as they saw themselves, fighting to liberate themselves from centuries of male domination, just as the blacks were fighting to free themselves from centuries of white domination; and the fight, since it had to be an organized fight, left no room for personal fulfillment. And since man as he had been and still continued to be was the enemy who had to be overcome, they became sexual warriors first, sexual lovers second if at all. For these women, who were by the late sixties identifying themselves as a new breed of feminists, even the word "man," in traditional English usage, had become an abomination. They were declaring themselves equal or superior to men, and demanding that, in sexual relationships, they have all the rights and privileges that men had previously enjoyed.

And the men, or at least nearly all of the men with liberal or radical leanings, the men whom Tom Robbins called "the androids," could hardly bring themselves to question, much less resist, the demands that the feminists were imposing on them. For these men their maleness was something to feel guilty about, like their whiteness. For them "make love not war" applied to women as well as Vietnam; and if the love did not always meet their expectations, and in fact often seemed more like making war than making love, particularly when they were being held up to new standards of sexual performance, that too must be the way sex had to be—in order to be free and equal. If, as one of my students confessed to me, the woman he loved wanted to have sex with other men, he had to be brave, even though he felt he was dying, and accept her activities with a cheerful countenance. If he did otherwise, he explained, he would be giving up on the possibility of sexual liberation for women. What she was doing to him, he added, was only what men had been doing to women for centuries.

Although not all men were as supine as this student, many of them were equally caught up in his guilt and his abstractions. When I pointed out that he could hardly take on the burden of all men's past mistreatment of women unless he wanted to turn himself into a sexual Christ, he could hardly understand what I was saying. To entertain any such idea as I was suggesting would, he responded, be to act like a sexist pig and impose his selfish wants and desires on the woman he loved. No, he continued, he would have to take her advice and learn to have sex with other women as she had sex with other men. Then the two of them would have a beautifully free and equal relationship that would also be sexually fulfilling.

How this particular relationship turned out I never learned, perhaps because my response was not what the student had expected. For I could not help saying that, from my point of view, sexual liberation was not liberation when it treated sex as a means to social ends, no matter how desirable those ends might seem. What finally was the difference between treating sex as it had been treated by the Church, as a means of procreation, and treating it as a way to achieve equality for women? The social ends were different but both treatments denied sexual fulfillment as an end in itself. And sex for kicks, or recreational sex, I added, also denied sexual fulfillment by turning sex into a game which any two or more participants could play—a game which Masters and Johnson and all the other sexual mechanics had turned into clinics based on the presumption that people are sex machines.

The gay and lesbian aspects of the movement I also had difficulty in accepting. Not homosexuality as such. I had long since come to accept the fact that homosexuality is neither a disease nor an aberration; that it is, on the positive side, a sexual difference which holds as much possibility for sexual fulfillment as heterosexuality—as proved by the lives of the many homosexuals I had read about or known personally. I could, moreover, sympathize fully with those homosexual individuals who were seizing upon the sexual movement as a means of achieving their own liberation. But the organized efforts of the gays and lesbians, it seemed to me, tended more towards conquest than liberation.

When I said something like this to a homosexual friend, his answer was brief and to the point: "What do you expect? We've been locked in the closet, persecuted and tormented when we've ventured out, and now you expect us to be good little fairies like your hero E. M. Forster. But we're out now, and we've got a chance, and we're going to make the most of it—legally and every other way. And if a few squares get trampled or seduced they've got it coming. Maybe, after we've got our rights and our dignity, we can be like E. M. Forster. But not till then." All this I found quite moving since it was said with genuine feeling, but I could not see that it made any more sense than the arguments of the feminists or the blacks. And his final point—that they would cease their organized aggression once they achieved their liberation—I could not accept for a moment, since it failed to take into account the nature of organizations and aggression. Organizations do not wither away, any more than the Communist state did. Specific organizations may die, but in dying, they invariably spawn their successors.

As for the gay and lesbian and feminist organizations they were already spawning all kinds of aberrant sexual groups and activities which they might honestly try to disown but which were bound to accompany their campaigns. If sex was to be freed, why not free it all? Whips, chains, bestiality, the whole works! And the organized liberators had no convincing answers. Or if they did I never encountered any. Norman Mailer's journalistic agonizings, in which he tries to decide whether, in portraying a sexual scene on the stage (or perhaps it was in a movie), the actors should actually copulate, comes to mind as one of the most absurd attempts of this kind that I read—not because it is unintelligent or inept in its argument but because it treats the question as if it were meaningful, or could somehow be made meaningful through historical and literary references.

In any event the questions that were worrying the liberators, as not only the media but the arts began cashing in on the new freedom, did not cause me any great concern. So long as sex was being used and sold I failed to see that it mattered greatly how it was being done. Soft porn or hard porn, whips or chains, power sex or recreational sex—they were all, as I saw them, either denials or perversions of the primary sexual impulses that they were ostensibly trying to free. Moreover they were becoming so powerful, so all-pervasive, that I began to wonder how long it would be possible for individuals to express their sexual impulses in one-to-one relationships having little if anything to do with power or recreation. In other words, I was wondering, good Freudian and Lawrentian that I was in such matters, how long Connie would be able to find her Mellors or Mellors find his Connie.

vii

The ideas and attitudes which I have been presenting in capsule form I discussed more systematically and at much greater length in essays I wrote at the time on D. H. Lawrence, George Orwell, and Victorian and modern love. "George Orwell: Our Responsible Quixote," appeared in the *West Coast Review*; "*Lady Chatterley's Lover*: A *Pilgrim's Progress* For Our Time," in *Paunch*; the others I circulated only in mimeographed form until, in 1968, James Flynn, Gerald Butler, and Evelyn Butler, all graduate students, formed a corporation and published these essays, along with a selection of my earlier ones, in a mimeographed book entitled, *Towards A Contextualist Aesthetic of the Novel* (Genitron Books, Inc., Seattle, 1968). By any standard theirs was an amazing accomplishment: mimeographing 255 single-spaced pages was a feat in itself, and their editorial work, considering the circumstances, was excellent. They wanted to bring together essays, critiques, and reviews which would show how I had been developing my critical ideas and practices into a contextualist aesthetic of the novel, and, given what they had to work with, they could hardly have done a better job. I was, and still am, more proud of the book than if it had been published by a commercial press.

The reviews of the book, all by former students, I was also quite proud of. Michael Steig, in his review (*The Minnesota Review*, 1968, pp. 376–379), subjected my criticism to the kind of analysis that I could understand and appreciate, even when, as was often the case, Steig found himself dissatisfied with my work. And I was of course pleased with his opening statement:

> Wayne Burns has probably had a greater influence upon students of literature than any other professor at the University of Washington in the past two decades. This influence is behind the founding of at least one journal of criticism and comment, *Paunch* (edited by Arthur Efron), from which, incidentally, Genitron promises a two-volume anthology soon. It is also behind the founding of Genitron Books, which will be moving

beyond the mimeographed format of this, its first volume. It would be, as the editors remark, a shame if readers were not to look behind the amateurishness with which this volume has been produced, for it is decidedly to the discredit of the academic and critical establishments that Professor Burns's work is so little known.

Pleased as I was, however, I could no longer share Steig's feeling that it was "to the discredit of the academic and critical establishments" that my work was not better known. The establishment, as I saw it, could let nothing in that it could not absorb: it knew what it wanted; it knew I was not providing what it wanted; and it would not accept me until I did. Not that I considered my own case in any sense special. The literary establishment could not accept anyone who did not provide what it wanted. In certain instances it might seem to, since its terms of acceptance, especially in its more radical wings, were really quite broad. Yet there was always a cut-off point. There had to be, unless the establishment was going to risk disestablishing itself, or, at the very least, embarrassing itself. Although I was, for instance, quite willing to have Leonard and Eleanor Manheim include "The Panzaic Principle" in a collection of psychoanalytic criticism they were editing, I felt sure they would have difficulty in getting it past a publisher's editor. And I was right. When their volume was finally accepted for publication under the title, *Hidden Patterns* (1966), it was with the stipulation that "The Panzaic Principle" not be included—for the very good reason that it did not fit into the hidden patterns of the book.

The Manheims, as my good friends, were upset, but I could by this time see and accept the workings of the literary establishment. What it wanted, in so far as it wanted anything new or different, was something just a trifle new, or a trifle different, a new twist on an old pattern that would provide a bit of excitement without raising ultimate questions about art and culture. Or, more directly, it wanted Ian Watt's *Rise of the Novel* or

Wayne Booth's *Rhetoric of Fiction*. And "The Panzaic Principle" was not like that, could not be made to appear like that. The better I or anyone stated it the less tolerable the establishment would find it.

Once again it may seem that I was putting myself on a Romantic pedestal from which I could then hurl anathemas at those who refused to accept my critical views. And I must once again affirm that I was doing no such thing. I was merely acknowledging what I knew to be true: that I could no more meet the establishment's literary or cultural demands than I could meet its social or political demands; that if I tried to re-phrase the Panzaic principle in terms the establishment could accept, the principle would be reduced to a critical truism, or worse still, to a critical adjunct to one or another of the many versions of body-worship prevalent in the late sixties.

For many of my students or former students who shared these views, my intransigence created a serious dilemma. Lack-ing my experience in such matters, and, in some instances, having a more sanguine temperament than mine, they believed that it might still be possible to storm the bastions of the literary establishment and prove that they were right. Arthur Efron, in *Paunch*, was fighting it out with everyone who took issue with the Panzaic, and seemingly winning all the battles if not the war. In *Paunch* number 25, for example, he wrote quite lengthy replies to Ian Watt, William Empson, and E. B. Greenwood. For my part, however, I could no longer see any hope in such ex-changes. While I could sympathize with Efron and others who engaged in them, I myself had come to feel that trying to discuss the Panzaic with anyone committed to any part of the establish-ment was almost certain to be an exercise in futility.

viii

I knew, however, that the Panzaic, as I had defined it, lent itself to serious misunderstandings; and I set about correcting them in a second essay ("The Panzaic Principle Part II") in

which I first of all tried to show that what is generally considered realistic in fiction cannot be equated with the Panzaic:

> No thing or being in fiction can be Panzaic in itself or in him-
> self. Not even a belly! Not even a phallus! A phallus, presented
> clinically, may be just a spout to urinate through; or, presented
> pornographically, it may be an object to thrill to. It is only
> Panzaic when it functions in such a way as to cut through what
> Ortega has described as the "crystalline orb of the ideal"—the
> way the pig's pizzle in Hardy's *Jude the Obscure*, for example, cuts
> directly through the crystalline orb of Jude's daydreams to show
> the phallic reality that underlies them—the reality that is to
> make a shambles of his ideals.

In this connection I also had to point out that my concept of the
Panzaic was not dependent on my interpretation of Sancho
Panza as a character in *Don Quixote*. Rather, I explained, my
aim was to identify a type of character common to innumerable
novels, a type which I had labelled Panzaic because, in my
opinion, Sancho Panza is the first and perhaps the most successful embodiment of the type. I could be wrong about Sancho, I
argued, and it still would not follow that I was wrong about the
type, which exists apart from Sancho and my application of his
name. Indeed the type could just as well be identified through
one or another of its twentieth-century exemplifications—
through, for example, Schweik in *The Good Soldier Schweik*, or
Zorba in *Zorba the Greek*, or the mother in Vittorini's *Conversation in Sicily*, or Kitten in Robert Gover's *One Hundred Dollar
Misunderstanding*.

Then, after discussing the ways in which these Panzaic characters function in their respective novels, I went on to conclude:

> What makes her [Kitten] and the other characters Panzaic,
> then, is not their outward or even their inward characteristics; it
> is their function—which is, as I have explained, to show that the
> senses of even a fool can give the lie to the noblest ideals of even
> the most profound thinker. But this, of course, does not mean
> that the Panzaic character must be a fool (although many of the

greatest have been); nor does it mean that the Panzaic character, by virtue of his giving the lie to the hero or heroine, then usurps the position of the hero or heroine and becomes a hero or heroine on his own.

The Panzaic is not synonymous with the sexual, or the Dionysian, or the Rabelaisian, or the Lawrentian, or, for that matter, any of the current forms of Zen or Hippie philosophizing. The Panzaic principle is *not* an attempt to elevate or idealize the Panzaic or Panzaic characters . . . By their very nature Panzaic characters cannot be so elevated—and still remain Panzaic. Inevitably they become heroic. And when this happens they can no longer function like Sancho Panza or like Schweik. They cease being undercutters of the ideal and become embodiments of the ideal, *i.e.*, they cease being Sancho Panzas and become spiritual Sancho Panzas or sensual Don Quixotes or, more positively, Tristans or Don Juans.

To illustrate this crucial distinction I chose as my first example *Lady Chatterley's Lover*, pointing out that Mellors is not, for all his Panzaic features, a Panzaic character. He is rather, I maintained, a hero, in a sense that none of Lawrence's other major novels have heroes; he is, in short, Lawrence's idealized self-image, a sensual Don Quixote with no Sancho Panza to challenge his sensual pretensions. For that reason the sexual scenes at times verge on sexual farce, and if the novel still manages to give the lie to "the insentient iron world," as I believe it does, it is through the exercise of prophetic powers that no other twentieth-century novelist has been able to generate. In any case those who have tried to follow Lawrence's example in *Lady Chatterley's Lover* seem to have mistaken Mellors for Lawrence. By transforming the Panzaic into the heroic, they have invariably ended up presenting more and more body, with more and more sex, in the hope that somehow it will mean something. But of course it never does. Either it is sensual and sentimental Quixoticism or, worse still, it degenerates into the murder, rape and suicide which Lawrence himself described in his much-quoted letter to Aldous Huxley, apropos of Huxley's efforts in *Point Counterpoint* to write a Lawrentian novel:

Intellectual appreciation does not amount to so much, it's what you thrill to . . . if you can only palpitate to murder, suicide, and rape, in their various degrees—and you state plainly that it is so—*caro*, however are we going to live through the days? Preparing still another murder, suicide, and rape? But it becomes of a phantasmal boredom and produces ultimately inertia, inertia, inertia and final atrophy of the feelings. Till, I suppose, comes a final super-war, and murder, suicide, rape sweeps away the vast bulk of mankind.

The distinction Lawrence draws here, I pointed out, is a crucial one: murder, suicide, and rape neither express nor appeal to our feelings or animal impulses; nor can they, when they are presented shockingly, or sensationally, or titillatingly, as in the movie version of Lawrence's *The Fox*, function Panzaically:

The movie version of D. H. Lawrence's *The Fox* grossly oversimplifies Lawrence's novella in order to achieve the same type of sensational appeal [as the movie, *A Man and a Woman*]. Will Banford win March? Or will Henry? Does March like homosexual love-making best? or heterosexual? or maybe she really prefers the fox? It is indeed a titillating triangle (or quadrangle, if we include the fox), especially as the movie makers exploit its possibilities, finally to resolve the conflict by means of a long drawn out second murder (Henry's killing the fox is, in the movie, the first murder) that presumably assuages March's doubts. In short, the movie is an unintended parody of the novella in everything from its sexiness to its symbol mongering. For the novella is not about sex or murder at all, it is about the man-woman relationship between March and Henry.

To show more fully how sex and murder deny or invert the Panzaic I chose Hubert Selby's *Last Exit to Brooklyn*, in part because a number of students had mistaken it for a Panzaic novel; in part because, in the quantity and quality of its sex and murder, it went beyond anything I had ever read; and in part because it provided the most clear-cut example I had yet found of a serious novel which used sex and murder not just to deny but to effect a complete inversion of the Panzaic principle. The characters in this novel, I tried to demonstrate, are not speaking or acting from their senses; they have no senses to speak or act from. Their feelings, paraphrasing Lawrence, have long since been atrophied. They might just as well be named "envy," "lust," "greed," etc., like characters in a medieval play. As for their fucking, heterosexual and homosexual, which takes up page after page in the novel, it is invariably a cold-hearted attempt to get something or prove something. Hardy's copulating earthworms in *Jude the Obscure* are warm in comparison. It is not until the fucking verges on rape and murder, as it does in almost every instance, that Selby's prose really begins to palpitate—and, if one may judge by the comments of reviewers, really begins to give his readers something to palpitate to. And such palpitations, I concluded, cannot give the lie to anything, although they can be used rhetorically, as Selby uses them, to invert the Panzaic and justify the invocation of Christian ideals.

I could, of course, have chosen a more highly-regarded novel for my prime illustration. I did in fact go on to discuss, much more briefly, a number of other novels (*The Stranger*, *Doctor Zhivago*, *One Flew Over The Cuckoo's Nest*, *Catch-22*, and *The Tin Drum*) in which I found the novelists evading or denying or expressing the Panzaic. But my aim was not to criticize individual novels; it was to clarify the workings of the Panzaic principle, to show that it has to be there if novels are to continue to realize Ortega's fears and Lawrence's hopes.

ix

The effect of this essay, as I circulated it in mimeographed form, was to separate me still further from the prevailing attitudes of the late sixties. Many of the graduate students who had been sympathetic to the Panzaic as I presented it in Part I were taken aback by my insisting, in Part II, that the Panzaic could never be identified with any form of body-worship; and, more disastrous still for many of them, my insisting that the Panzaic could never, under any circumstances, become the heroic. Yet their reactions were nothing like as intense as those of the undergraduates. By this time many of them were either committed to or thrilling to the "sexual revolution," and to them my Part II seemed like a denial of what they had found in Part I. Or, as one of them put it, "a cop out." As for my colleagues, their perception of the Panzaic did not seem to change. Nor did I expect it to. What I found difficult to accept was the fact that the liberal and radical students who had formerly been willing to give my views on life and literature a sympathetic hearing were now inclined to dismiss them as cranky or even reactionary.

x

My difficulties on the faculty level also increased when, in 1965 or '66, the department began scrapping its old system of Ph.D. exams in which students first wrote for three days on a critical essay, a genre question, and Chaucer, Milton, and Shakespeare, plus twelve other major figures of their own choice; and then, after a period of several weeks, defended what they had written in a three-hour oral exam. As such examinations go, it was, I am convinced, one of the best ever devised. Admittedly it was cumbersome, and made demands on the professors involved which were perhaps inordinate, but those were not the primary reasons for scrapping it. The ostensible reason derived from the silly statistics that someone, somewhere, had come up with—statistics which indicated that in a very few years there would be a dearth of Ph.D.'s, that consequently the students who would then be flooding the universities would be without adequately prepared teachers. Where these statistics came from no longer matters. The point is that the department, and presumably the University, took them seriously, or at any rate used them as a reason for gearing up to meet these projected demands.

The form the gearing-up took, however, left no doubt that there were other reasons at work. For the new exams reverted back to the old style "writtens" and "orals," with far more emphasis on literary periods and on conventional scholarship and criticism—in a word, far more emphasis on regurgitation in the name of knowledge. The students now had to learn by rote the facts which the professors expected them to know. And when many of them still did not measure up, the department introduced graduate survey courses which would "prep" them for the exam—survey courses which, in effect, became mandatory, since it was almost impossible for a student to do well on the exam without taking them. From my point of view it was a sorry business, made sorrier by its effects on graduate students. No longer could they afford the luxury of taking courses that did not point towards the exam, or, in my own case, courses that pointed away from it. A few still did, whether they could afford to or not, but they were always a bit nervous in doing so. For they had to confront still another pressure which the department imposed at this time when it stressed that all candidates for the Ph.D. were expected to complete the degree within four years, not the five or six or seven that most of the students I worked with had taken.

To complete the reorganization, the department also devised a new system for supervising and evaluating Ph.D. theses. From the first I suspected that one of the aims of the new system was to put my work as a supervisor under stricter faculty control, and my suspicions were soon borne out by the comments that seeped through the grapevine—to the effect that the department was tired of running a graduate school so that I could take over some of the best students and lead them through sexual exercises which had less to do with scholarship and criticism than with what was taking place on campus. As these comments indicate, a good bit of the rancor which some of my colleagues were coming to feel towards me during these years derived, paradoxically enough, from their identifying me with the sexual revolution that I, for different reasons, deplored as much as they did.

But that kind of misunderstanding no longer affected me very seriously nor did the new machinery affect my supervising as much as I had feared it would. I continued to have students working with me on their theses, and they continued to get through—thanks in large measure to the fact that the old openness, the old freedom, had not yet been fully organized out of the department. There were still too many professors who, if they were not as unhappy with the new machinery (and what it represented) as I was, were at least unhappy enough to persist in their old attitudes, their old ways. They might teach "prep" surveys, yet they often apologized to the students for doing so; they might administer the new exams, yet they often failed to exercise the rigor that the system demanded; they might serve on thesis committees, yet they were as reluctant as ever to outlaw the Panzaic or anything else outrageous as long as it made sense. It was all I could ask, and it enabled me to continue this phase of my graduate teaching with almost as much success as I had enjoyed in earlier years.

xi

My classroom teaching, on the other hand, went less and less well during these years on both the graduate and undergraduate level. In my undergraduate classes a great part of the difficulty had to do with the fact that I had come to stand in a different relationship to the students and their liberal causes and ideals. Although I myself had never been a liberal by profession I had, I suppose, been one by default, since my radical beliefs, first as a would-be Marxist and then as an anarchist, had led me to subscribe, or seem to subscribe, to the whole gamut of liberal beliefs—from pacifism to women's rights. And while I always tried to make it clear that I could not, as a parasitic anarchist, espouse these beliefs in the way liberals did, my demurrers never seemed to have much effect on the students. After all I was still on the right side, and if I wanted to go to extremes they could put up with that, especially since my extremes always led me to be far more critical of conservative beliefs than of liberal ones. For the most part, therefore, it was the more conservative students who found my views wholly unacceptable, and since they were few in number in my classes and for the most part unable or unwilling to put up much resistance, no matter how much I encouraged them, I seldom had to confront outright ideological hostility.

Then, almost overnight, the mood of the students changed. At first I could hardly believe what was happening. For over twenty years I had been questioning the students' beliefs and ideals, and because I had not, in my questioning, been attacking them, they had been willing to go along with me. Or at least some of them had been willing to go along, and the rest had been willing to put up with what they dismissed as my eccentric negativism. Then the new movements began to take over the campus: bullhorns were blaring; the halls of the student union building were bursting with literally dozens of stalls filled with the literature of dozens of causes; students were carrying placards or meeting on steps or in conference rooms; and members of the faculty were either joining in discreetly or looking on with benevolence or apprehension. These were just the beginnings of the campus turmoil—the riots and police brutality came later—yet they were sufficient in themselves to transform the great majority of the students from scoffers or seekers to guardians of the faith.

I first became aware of the transformation when, in the opening sessions of my classes, the students began to meet my teasingly satirical references to bicycles and backpacks with unusually stony silence. I had always, since I first began teaching, used such references, applying them to one or another of the cultish habits of the day in an effort to lead gently into the more serious discussions to follow. And usually, since the students would already have a fairly well-developed sense of what was cultish, and how ridiculous certain aspects of the cultish could be, the tactic would help me to establish some kind of rapport with the class. The students would begin to realize that I was not attacking them, only certain of their habits and attitudes about which they themselves had doubts. But somewhere in the middle sixties they ceased having doubts, or their doubts became so strong that they could no longer tolerate having them taken lightly. In one class, after having one or two dismal opening sessions in which the students had seemed reluctant to find anything interesting or amusing in my likening some of the national leaders of the ecological movement to cosmic cheerleaders, I thought I might break the tension by putting a few silly verses on the board:

> Rah! Rah! Environment!
> Let's make it Permanent
> In our great big Firmament!

Maybe one or two people in the class smiled, but for the rest it was as if I had desecrated their church.

And when, in that class and others, more serious questions came up for discussion, the resistance often deepened into thinly disguised hostility. I discovered that not just my words and phrases but those in the novels we were reading no longer had meaning, or carried meanings for the students that they could no longer consider with equanimity. I am not now referring to the more obvious and serious questions of nomenclature, such as the blacks wishing to be called "blacks" instead of "Negroes," but to such everyday words as "selfish" or "style" or "homely." A student's finding fault with my use of "homely" puzzled me the most, as I recall, since I failed to see how there could be any objection to the word, as word, unless it were applied to someone unfeelingly or unfairly. Nor was I much enlightened when the student declared that no one could be "homely" regardless of how he looked; and then went on to add, when I asked him what he called those were were less good-looking than others, that such people would simply be "less beautiful." At this juncture, I should have retreated, particularly since the class seemed to share the student's notion that "homely" had meanings too negative for any further use, but I ventured one more question: "Do you have a word for those who are much less beautiful?"— a question which, for all its pertinence, merely served to confuse and alienate the student, and, as far as I could tell, the class.

I mention this particular episode because, though trivial in itself, it shows how thoroughly most of the students had politicized themselves. They had not been brainwashed, in the ordinary sense of that term; they had, through their own insecurities and fears of group pressure, brainwashed themselves. Outwardly they had nothing to fear but the disapproval of the more zealous among their fellow students. No leader, to the best of my knowledge, was telling them, except in a very general way, how they should respond to the edicts of the SDS or the Black Student Union; they were doing it to themselves and to each other. Nor was anyone telling them, as the McCarthyites had told good citizens earlier, that they must seek out and expose the enemy, or risk being mistaken for the enemy themselves. No, they created their own McCarthyism, the McCarthyism of the student left.

I am not, in so far as I understand my own terminology, being rhetorical. McCarthyism of the student left is, I am convinced, an accurate descriptive phrase as it applies to those students who were trying to bully their professors and fellow students into compliance with ideological beliefs which could neither be questioned nor opposed in rational terms. In my own classes, however, it was not the bullying itself which did the greatest damage but the atmosphere of hostility and fear and mistrust which the bullying created—an atmosphere in which no one could speak except in defensive or offensive terms, an atmosphere which turned many of my classes during those years into nothing more than trials of strength. It was me against them, with the students who were genuinely interested in what I was trying to get at obliged to stop by after class, or look me up in my office or in my coffee sessions. In some classes the resistance took the form of sullen silence, broken only by the desultory questions of the students who were still worried about grades. On these occasions, despite my conviction that there was no excuse for lecturing, I came close to doing just that—until I discovered my own variation on an old rhetorical technique. I would pose the questions that I knew were in the students' minds and then conduct an imaginary dialogue in which I was alternately student and professor. And if I struck just the right chords in my imaginary dialogues I could sometimes stir the class into grudging participation. But it was a gruelling, grinding process, with no joy or meaning in it either for me or for the few students who understood and sympathized with what I was attempting, and for the first time in my life I began to wonder whether I wanted to keep on doing it.

The classes in which I encountered more open hostility posed somewhat different problems, as, for instance, when one student, participating in a discussion of *1984* that had somehow got onto ecology and whales, told me in quite pointed terms that if he had a choice between saving me or a whale he would choose the whale because it was an endangered species and I was not. While he could have said this in a maner which would not have been offensive, (the way, for example, the student I mentioned earlier had told me I was "a great big phony") there was no mistaking his tone, or his manner. And I, forgetting for a moment that I had to recognize the circumstances and exercise special restraint, responded by pointing out that no doubt Hitler thought the Aryans were an endangered species, that whenever anyone started sacrificing individuals to abstract concepts, such as "an endangered species," there was no limit to where he might end up. What I was saying was fair enough, I believe, although it was the wrong time to say it, and I had a few anxious moments later as to where I myself might end up. For other members of the class, who had up to this point been sitting on their hostilities, gave vent to them in a verbal onslaught which I barely managed to control. One student wanted to know whether I put my life ahead of any cause, and when I answered that I did, that I not only put mine but his, other students entered in to charge me with everything from being selfish, individualist, elitist, and male chauvinist, to being an anarchist as well as an authoritarian. The words themselves I did not mind. Students had been inveighing against my views in pretty much the same terms right along. But their spirit had been different: they had been attacking my views, or my interpretations, not me; and in answering them I had therefore been able to clarify my position, and hopefully theirs, without defending myself or attacking them. I was a person, they were persons; I had my views and interpretations; they had theirs. But my views and interpretations were not me; their views and interpretations were not them. And so we could have intellectual discussions. But what took place in this class was altogether different: it was a personal attack, in response to what the students had mistaken for personal attacks on them. It was as if I had become the embodiment of everything they feared and hated. And it was dreadful, not only for me but for them and for those in the class who were not directly involved. My years in the classroom stood me in good stead, however, and I finally managed to get myself and the class through the hour with a semblance of sanity. But the class, as a class, never recovered: from that point until the end of the quarter they and I were simply marking time.

One of my friends on the faculty, when I told him about the incident, offered the obvious solution: "Throw the guys out for disrupting the class. That's what I would have done." But that solution could never work for me. If I threw the students out I would in effect be throwing myself out, since my entire approach to teaching was based on the premise that the students had to be able to express themselves freely; and if any number of them were in such a state that they could not possibly do that without overstepping the bounds of intellectual discussion there was nothing I could do but try to keep the lid on and hope for the best.

That was also how I had to proceed when I encountered hostility in the form of student vigilantes. On one occasion, after I had referred in class to something one of the feminist leaders on campus had said, I was surprised to find a strange contingent of feminists sitting in my next class and insisting that I account for my remarks of the previous day in which I had taken their leader's words so lightly. At this point I can hear some of my colleagues saying: "But I never had anything like that happen to me. You must have been looking for trouble.

Why couldn't you just be discreet until the students came to their senses?" The answer, needless to say, was the same answer I had been obliged to give again and again, from boyhood onwards, when others asked me essentially the same question. I had never learned how to be discreet, even when I wanted to be. And there came a time, with the students, when I no longer wanted to be.

I could not believe, as so many of my colleagues did, that the hysteria would pass and all would be as well or better than before. What was happening to me and everyone could not be temporary: much of it was already being accepted and institutionalized. In 1966 or '67 the Associated Students Union, with the approval of the University, issued its first *Course Critique* in which the students rated the professors A, B, C, D and commented on their abilities as teachers. One member of the English department who had for years been having a difficult time getting his work published and accepted and had tried to console himself in the belief that he was a good teacher—a belief, by the way, that was fully warranted—not only received a low rating by the students but a series of comments which, as I understand it, he found devastating—so devastating that he committed suicide.

Now I am not suggesting that the critique alone drove my colleague to suicide. But in the state I was in at the time I could understand how it might have such a dreadful effect. For I too, for quite different reasons, was coming to feel that the teaching which had meant so much to me for so long might be over—though not, I must hasten to add, because of the verdict passed on me by the *Critique*. Although I received a very low grade—a C— or perhaps even a D as I recall—along with mostly derogatory comments, neither the grade nor the comments proved very disturbing. Indeed I could not help feeling highly complimented by one student's plaintive remark: "He talks about sex all the time but he doesn't make it interesting." When such evaluations became institutionalized and mandatory, professors who did not conform to the students' demands would, I recognized, have to fight for their lives as teachers. But that was in the future. My fight was immediate.

The zealots among the would-be revolutionary students were running me right out of the classroom, the one place in my once heavenly city that had up to this time remained heavenly—the place that had over the years become my intellectual home; the place where, intellectually, and in some respects emotionally, I had lived most intensely and meaningfully; the place where I could always go and be sure of a sympathetic hearing for my ideas and perceptions when my efforts to communicate with my fellow academics or the outside world went awry. If the classroom had not always been there for me I could never have developed or expressed my critical ideas as I did, never have worked with students as I did. And it was all being destroyed by zealous kids whose revolutionary path would lead them straight into office jobs with Exxon or IBM.

Yet there seemed to be little if anything that I could do—except to continue to teach and speak out in the classroom as long as I could. A number of students, I knew, were still listening, even though they did not feel that they could express themselves freely in class. I knew all this because they continued to stop by my office or to join me and a few graduate students as we were having coffee. And when one of these students asked me, in February 1969, if I would meet with him and other students in an obscure coffee house to explain my sense of the situation on campus more directly, without the need for discretion imposed by the atmosphere in the classes, I agreed, observing at the same time, half-seriously, that I thought the conspiratorial nature of his arrangements seemed quite appropriate. The meeting itself, however, was not only open but taped, with the first hour consisting of an interview in which I responded to questions posed by a student, Doug Neal. Although what I said was not very different from what I had been saying in my classes, I perhaps said it less circumspectly—as, for instance, in my remarks at the beginning of the interview on the power struggle on campus:

Once the walls are down there will be no stopping the power seekers. Freedom will go, no matter who is in control. That is why I deplore any kind of power struggle. Isaiah Berlin has explained that freedom may not be compatible with justice or equality or democracy, that one may have to choose between two or more of these goods. And my own choice is freedom. On campus I don't want what various groups call justice or equality or democracy. I just want the freedom to keep on teaching the way I have been, and I might not be able to do this if, for instance, the students gained control. . . .

Why not?

Why? The university puts out a course critique in which students rate professors, and I received a "D" rating in their critique. It's like television: you put on a program and you get a mass rating. In fact I should describe all such ratings as upsurges of the mass mind.

Then, towards the end of the hour, the student interviewer commented:

Mr. Burns, you have penetrated a lot of areas which are standard, accepted modes of life and education in particular. Only very few people can share your views on today's higher education and no more than a handful may be aware of many of the things that you have struck at.

Actually you seem to believe that a very individualistic role is necessary to the true survival of education—or society, for that matter. Can you give us some final comments on that assessment?

And in my final comments, after reviewing some of the things I had been saying, I reaffirmed my anarchist position:

Actually I don't think you can speak of the survival of education or society apart from the survival of individuals. For my part I feel no concern for the survival of even . . . the university, except in so far as it sustains and nourishes individual students and teachers. . . .

To ask, or to demand, or to expect that a University of some 30,000 students can be humanized is to me sheer naivete. And to persist in this demand or expectation is sheer folly, and can only lead to still further institutionalization of students and teachers alike.

What all factions have got to realize eventually is that justice and equality do not mean freedom. The Black Power movement doesn't realize this any more than the white political machinery. John Stuart Mill and De Tocqueville have tried to tell us that Democracy may be the greatest tyrannical force we have going— especially American democracy. Just examine our history. Or read Dickens' *American Notes* and *Martin Chuzzlewit.* Or just look around you . . . At the Hippies, for example, who are as groupy and as a groovey as the jet set. Or the SDS'ers and their "organization." Or those incredible young men and women who call themselves "Youth for Democracy." Despite all the political fuss and resistance—much of which I sympathize with—we get groupier all the time. We have "group therapy" as destructive of individualism as anything the communists ever devised; and we can't even recognize that "sensitivity training" (which is of course another group project) is a contradiction in terms; or that "doing your own thing" will turn you into a thing, just like doing your job will.

But in the university—if the university can survive—it is possible to mark these distinctions. And, on the positive side, it is still possible to cherish one's individual freedom and to culti-vate one's individual differences. This is why I am an anarchist and a professor.

The students were quite enthusiastic, and I was also pleased to learn, a bit later, that Doug Neal had transcribed his tapes of the interview for an underground newspaper in Seattle—a tran-scription which I mimeographed for my classes under the title, "As the Walls Come Tumbling Down: A View from the Ivory Tower." Further developments from the meeting also seemed to indicate that, if I were so inclined, I might perhaps become the leader of still another campus faction—one calling itself, say, "Youth for Anarchistic Action." But a leader was the last thing I wanted to become. There were already too many leaders and too many followers. I had no desire to capture the University; I only wanted to recapture my own classroom.

xii

In my graduate classes the effects of the campus revolution were less dramatic. While the graduate students had also taken to jeans and backpacks and bicycles, and held much the same beliefs as the undergraduates, they did not hold them with anything like the same fervor. The feminists among them at times came close to matching the zeal of their undergraduate sisters, but with the exception of one group that I encountered, in one fateful seminar, they too were inclined to be tolerant.

In some respects, indeed, my views were much to the feminists' liking, since I had for years been maintaining that women in fiction were, with hardly any exceptions, far more interesting, far more "round" in Forster's sense of the term, than men. On occasion I put it even more bluntly: that the male characters were usually dolts in comparison with the women. Moreover I argued, and believed, that this was true for male novelists as well as women novelists. The feminists, needless to say, were pleased; and they were even more pleased when I went on to observe, as I invariably did, that the superiority of women in fiction might seem to derive from their being superior in life. Yet the more perceptive among the feminists were also a bit uneasy, in part, I suppose, because they doubted my sincerity, but also because, in my discussions of this phenomenon, I went outside of or crossed over the lines that they were accustomed to draw. Women's claims of physical superiority in athletics, for instance, I could not even take seriously. And I acknowledged that I had difficulty in seeing why, being superior creatures in what counted most, they wished to give that up in an effort to become superior in what counted least, especially when they could have equal pay, and all the other equalities they wanted and deserved without becoming female versions of men. At this point, for the more sophisticated among them, the name of Freud, their *bête noir*, would flash through their minds, or if not Freud, D. H. Lawrence, another *bête noir*, and they would tend to see everything I had been saying as a complex putdown. To their credit, however, they were usually willing to express their doubts about me and the Panzaic in terms that made for meaningful discussion.

The graduate students who were committed to the other phases of the campus revolution were, for the most part, less militant than the feminists, primarily, I think, because they were more confused. On the one hand they wanted to believe in everything the new liberals and radicals were promulgating, and in one sense most of them did; on the other hand they wanted to hold onto the critical theories and practices which they had grown up with—theories and practices which were, if examined at all closely, totally incompatible with the social-political beliefs they were trying to profess. How could they, I questioned, profess these beliefs and still, in matters literary, hew to the by now old critical lines represented by Northrop Frye? If they were prepared to concede any connection whatsoever between literature and life they would, I argued, have to do some reconsidering—if not along Panzaic lines, then along those which were being set forth by, for example, the New Marxists. My aim of course was to get the students to recognize their dilemma. And a few of them did. But that was the last thing most of them were prepared to do. Either they rationalized their inconsistencies or they took refuge in an alternative which might be called the new cynicism. I called it new, even though it was philosophically ancient, because they simply refused to acknowledge its philosophical implications, dismissing Stephen Pepper's analysis of utter scepticism, when I called it to their attention, as no longer relevant. Pepper might argue that "an utter skeptic . . . turns into a dogmatist" but that, they insisted, was just another philosophical argument. Northrop Frye might be incompatible with the campus revolution, but who worried about incompatibility, or even inconsistency. One could reject Frye the social philosopher, who leaned heavily on Matthew Arnold, and still recognize Frye as a fine and sensitive critic. After all, criticism was not philosophy, or aesthetics, but a game, a profession. For that matter, art itself was a game, literature was a game. Surely everyone in graduate school knew this; surely the professors knew it; surely I knew it.

While they were right, of course, about everyone knowing it, their argument carried the further implication that everyone was doing it; and that it was, if not good, at least inevitable that everyone do it. Since this meant that I was doing it too, I tried to challenge them directly by pointing out that, if they gave me credit for having any sense of what I was attempting or doing, they must recognize that I could hardly be playing a game. For one thing, no one could be stupid enough, if he were playing a game, to do what I was doing. But this argument seldom convinced the new cynics: if I were an attorney, they argued, I would have to play the game of law, whatever my motives in playing it. The same if I were a doctor, or a composer, or a scientist. Freud was playing a game, Lawrence was playing a game! And was Jesus Christ playing a game, I asked, or Gandhi? These two gave them pause, but only for a moment: Do you think, then, that you are Jesus Christ as English professor? Or Gandhi? To which I had to reply: I think I may be closer to them than to the game players, and I am certain that Freud and Lawrence were. But that did not faze them. There were, they declared, bound to be a few nuts who either were not playing or failed to realize that they were.

The implications of their argument, taken seriously, were staggering. As it applied to me it meant that all my fuss about the Panzaic was pointless: how could the Panzaic undercut beliefs or ideals when they were no longer there to be undercut. For that matter how could the Panzaic undercut anything—except as a game. Nothing was left but the kicks or sensations, refined or not so refined, that could be got from playing the game of sex, or politics, or poetry, or pinochle. Poetry was a better game than pinochle: that was the only difference between the two. Nothing was real but the game, and the sensations, in money, sex, power, prestige that the game would yield. As for the Panzaic game, the new cynics were kind enough to say that they were willing to play it, although they did not find it as interesting as some of the others they had played, including the Northrop Frye games which I had disparaged.

My immediate problem, as I saw it, was how to confront this new cynicism without charging into its seemingly impenetrable defenses and insisting on implications that the individual cynics were really not ready to face. For I could sense, beneath their sophisticated bravado, the same kind of resistance to the Panzaic that I had been encountering in my undergraduate classes. Few of them wanted to be pushed very far: they were no longer in the mood for the kinds of discussion that threatened their composure. After all they had exams to pass—ridiculous exams, perhaps, but they had to pass them. And they had theses to write—theses that would meet the requirements of the scholarly-critical game and assure them a future in which they could continue to play it. These were their realities, and they had no patience with my comparing them to the realities of Tolstoy's Ivan Ilych, or making any other connections between their lives and literature.

Theoretically these new cynics should have been fundamentally at odds with the feminists and others who were more naively committed to the movements of the time, but in my classes the two groups seemed to form a united front against me and any students who seemed inclined to push the discussion of critical questions to the extremes I thought interesting. And so, in my graduate as in my undergraduate classes, I found myself struggling as I had never struggled before. Although graduate students were usually polite as well as tolerant there was no mistaking their resistance, which hung like a pall over my attempts to force at least some recognition of their new complacencies. At one point, in trying to define good teaching in "As The Walls Come Tumbling Down" I had said:

> Good teaching is many things—among others it's the art of wasting time. But it is not something that you can set up goals for, not something that you can program. It's something that happens—between the teacher and the students and the mater-

ial—and the good teacher is the one who makes this something happen as often as possible.

It was, I believe, a good if brief definition, and my own words were more and more coming back to haunt me. For I had to recognize that, given the kind of resistance I had been getting, I could no longer make this something happen.

One way to lessen the resistance, I thought, might be to offer a seminar based on the work I had been doing on Denis de Rougement's *Love in the Western World*. Leslie Fiedler had drawn heavily on de Rougement in his *Love and Death in the American Novel* and it looked to me as if de Rougement's work lent itself even more directly to Victorian fiction. Although the course I eventually worked out, "Love and Death in the Victorian Novel," necessarily involved sexual questions that might prove volatile, I had dealt with such questions innumerable times before in my graduate courses, and in any case I planned to approach the questions from a new and less provocative angle. The Panzaic would still be there, but I would be encouraging the students, via de Rougement, to explore the ways in which the Victorian novelists had sought to overcome it, including the ways in which one novelist, Emily Bronte, actually succeeded in overcoming it—by having Cathy and Heathcliff achieve, in death, the union that had been impossible to them in life.

Whatever hopes I had for the seminar were, however, dissipated in its very first meeting, in which seven or eight students, representing approximately half the class, took it upon themselves to question everything from the number of novels I had assigned to the procedures which I suggested that we follow in subsequent meetings. In all my years of teaching I had never encountered so much hostility in the opening session of a graduate class. And the hostility increased with every meeting, as a triumvirate of zealous feminists, aided and abetted by a group of three or four new cynics, tried to block my every attempt to initiate serious discussion of love and death in the novels under consideration. Under the guise of disinterested objectivity the students questioned every word that had sexual meanings or connotations. If I mentioned "passion" in a context which clearly indicated I was using the word as de Rougement defines it, one of the feminists would ask if I were speaking as a Freudian. Or if I said I was paraphrasing Freud one of them would ask if I were speaking as a Lawrentian. Childish as their gambits were, they were dreadfully effective—though apparently not effective enough. Not content to slow me and the class down to meaningless quibbling, they finally resorted to a strange kind of filibuster. The excuse for it came when, in discussing Charlotte Bronte's *Villette*, I suggested that the heroine's relish for dressing and acting as a man, even though she was acting in a play, had interesting lesbian implications. Somewhere in the discussion I had also used the word "transvestite," and that word, coupled with the word "lesbian," sent one of the feminists into a tirade which did not end, despite my going into a tirade of my own in an effort to stop it, until I dismissed the class.

Now conceivably the woman's tirade could have been real, in the sense that she had, like the woman in one of my earlier classes, made identifications which were terribly disturbing. Or she could have been acting, like the heroine she was trying to defend, and found herself overwhelmed by the emotions she was trying to act out. Or her performance could have been just straight acting. (A few weeks later, when she talked with me about the episode, she herself seemed confused about her feelings and motives.) But at the time, in the circumstances, after the weeks of harassment, I was in no mood to be charitable. I was a teacher, not a saint, and I had reached the limits of my endurance. At the next meeting of the seminar I read the following statement:

English 541   March 6, 1972

The kind of seminar I have been trying to conduct—in which I entertain various points of view but insist on presenting my own—is premised on mutual trust. You have to trust me to be honest and forthright in what I present; I have to trust you to be equally honest and forthright in what you present. But some of you, it would seem, never trusted me, even in the beginning: or if you did, the trust you had proved unequal to the rigors of discussion, and you apparently came to feel (consciously or unconsciously) that I was trying to put something over on you, trying to seduce you or browbeat you into accepting my contextualist aesthetic (along with my Sancho Panzism, Freudianism, etc.). I say "consciously or unconsciously" because I do not think any of you were consciously trying to get me, or do me in; rather you were, as I see it, trying to defend your beliefs and your values from what you conceived to be my unfair attempts to undermine them. And you consequently felt justified in trying to stop me.

All this I was aware of from the beginning: all this, throughout the quarter, I tried to make allowances for—even though, in doing so, I realized that our discussion could never go anywhere unless I could somehow overcome your feelings of resentment and suspicion. But I never could. And in our last meeting I stopped trying and voiced my protest, not only against your lack of trust in my personal and scholarly integrity but against the tactics you were using to obstruct the lines of discussion I had initiated. Even now, after several days of reconsideration, I cannot see how, in good conscience, I could have done anything but what I did. Perhaps, just perhaps, it even did some good. I sincerely hope so. But whatever the good, it comes too late to make any difference in what we can accomplish in these last two class meetings. So I am simply calling them off—though I shall be happy to stay and talk further about our difficulties or anything else you would like to talk about today. And I will be here again on Wednesday, to talk further about your individual term papers or anything else that you want to talk about. And of course I will see you on Monday afternoon for our final exam.

Even as I wrote this statement I knew that it was my swan song as a graduate teacher. I knew that it was because I also knew that I could have, and perhaps should have, read much the same statement in just about every graduate class I had taught for the past five or six years. Except for the unremitting zeal of the three feminists and the final tirade, what went on in this class was not a great deal worse than what had gone on in others—and would, I was convinced, continue to go on in every graduate class I would henceforth try to teach. As a teacher I had been defeated. I could go through the motions, but I could no longer make it happen.

8

On My Way to Early Retirement
(1972–1979)

From 1972 onwards I was constantly trying to come to terms with my defeat as a teacher. My obvious alternative, to resign my professorship and try to do something else, had considerable appeal for me—except that, as a practical matter, I could see the something else becoming more difficult for me than the University. After all, I had spent my entire life in universities, and I knew that leaving the academic world altogether, without having something else I really wanted to do, and felt sure I could do, would be just about impossible for me. I would have to find an alternative before I resigned, and since the alternative that intrigued me the most was also one that I could try experimentally in the summers, I chose that, despite the fact that I knew it to be, in economic terms, highly impractical.

I had always had a passion for boats and the sea, and had recently, through getting to know some of the local fishermen, gained new respect for the independent lives they seemed to be living. And while I could see drawbacks too, enormous ones in fact, I decided to give fishing a try. I bought and rebuilt a 91-foot boat that would double as a jig boat, trolling for albacore tuna off the West Coast, and as a fish-packer, a kind of sea-going truck used to pick up salmon from fishermen in local waters or in Alaska. Then, for the next five years, I spent my summers trying to become a fisherman. It took only a few albacore trips, rolling around in the huge swells a hundred miles off the coast, without adequate knowledge or experience, to convince me of the foolishness of that part of my venture. The fish-packing, on the other hand, went reasonably well, but in order to make a living at that I would, I had begun to see, have to sign up with one of the big fish companies and become a paid employee with a boat. The days of the independent fish-packer were numbered. In the circumstances, therefore, I had no choice but to sell the boat and get out of fishing—a wise decision on all counts, as it turned out, because the entire salmon fishery in the Northwest has since gone from bad to calamitous.

ii

My summers as a professional fisherman I have never regretted. For one thing I enjoyed them tremendously; for another they took so much time and energy that, for three or four months out of the year, I could forget what was happening in the University. And what was happening through the early and middle seventies was indeed sad, not only for me but for everyone in literature and the humanities. For if what I had been attempting had, in many respects, set me apart from nearly all my colleagues, they too, in different ways and for different reasons, were becoming casualties of the campus revolution and its aftermath. While the students might not try to sabotage their classes, they were doing what, from a departmental point of view, was even worse: they were staying away. Enrollments in English classes dropped alarmingly. The course in Victorian poetry, if I remember correctly, had at one point not enrolled a single student for over two years. Nor were some of the courses which had previously been turning students away much better off, despite the department's attempts to cater not only to the students' demands but to their whims.

One of the saddest caterings for me was the institutionaliza-tion of student evaluations. It can, of course, be argued that neither the University nor the English department had any real choice in the matter. Public as well as student pressure was too great for any institution to resist. But it was one thing for the department to bow to the inevitable, quite another for certain of its members to vie with one another in trying to justify the evaluations. One man whom I had always respected, in address-ing a departmental meeting, actually went so far as to say: "I know the evaluations don't measure anything significant but they are objective and that is why we must apply them. We can no longer afford to be subjective in our judgments." Although I myself did not answer this bit of academic double-think—I had not spoken in a meeting for years—I think perhaps someone did say, "God forbid that we be subjective and make sense; better that we be objective and measure accurately what doesn't matter."

Yet even that answer did not go far enough, for by measur-ing what had no significance, and subjecting themselves to the measurements, the members of the department were acknowl-edging their own insignificance—both as individuals and as teachers. For they knew that what the evaluations did measure, in almost every instance, was the professor's willingness to make himself and his courses agreeable to the students. If even a few students in a class were dissatisfied the "objective" evaluations (in answer to such questions as, "Does he make his subject clear and understandable?") would pull his rating for that class below the passing mark—which the department set at 7, on an "objec-tive" scale of 1 to 10. So everybody who expected to get a raise or a promotion or tenure had to get a bunch of 7-10's. I and one other member of the department whom I knew about chose not to participate, even when the evaluations became obliga-tory, and perhaps a few others did too. But nearly everyone complied. And pretty soon they were all, or nearly all, getting 7's or better.

But they had not become better teachers. At best they had become better simplifiers and packagers; at worst they had become academic disc jockeys, selling Chaucer, or Milton, or

Joyce instead of the Beatles or Bob Dylan or Simon and Garfunkel, but using an academic version of the same tactics. Great writers were relevant as well as enjoyable once you recognized that they were incipient feminists, or environmentalists, or anti-racists. The students could hardly be blamed: for nearly all of them 1965 marked the beginning of true knowledge. But the professors knew better. They knew they were becoming salesmen in order to get their 7–10 ratings; and they also knew, or at least many of them did, that they were marketing literature the way TV marketed beer. Their excuse always was that it had to be done in order to save literature and culture. There was always the possibility that if the students read literature they might get something besides slogans out of it.

Feeble as this argument was, it too had to be abandoned when, as enrollments continued to drop despite all the new gimmicks, the department had to start offering courses in popular fiction, children's literature, and science fiction—courses which were designed, purely and simply, to get more students—or, as they had come to be referred to, more FTE's, an administrative term which turned students into Full-Time Equivalents. Once again it can be argued that the department had no choice: unless these courses were offered, and generated more FTE's, the departmental budget would be cut, many professors would lose their jobs, and the department might no longer be able to market even such classics as Dickens and Thackeray.

While I could sympathize with this argument, I could also see its inescapable ramifications. Nor was I alone in my dire forebodings. On January 26, 1978, a mordant little satire appeared anonymously in the "English Department Newsletter of the University of Washington." The satire purports to be "Excerpts from a journal recording a visit to Futopia in the year 1998," and it reads in part:

On the third day of my tour of the University, I asked to visit the English Department.

"English Department?" said my guide, Brightaloft, in an in-
quiring tone. "What's that?" He pressed some buttons on the
console built into his desk, and on the screen flashed a wordlist
headed "Early Twentieth-Century Archaisms."

"Ay, yes," he said, "What we want is the Division of Expres-
sive Communication. What luck! One of their most popular
classes is just beginning."

Before you could say "Jules Verne," he had activated our
Topographical Transformers, and we found ourselves in an
enormous hall where hundreds of young people were seated in
rows, waiting for the session to begin.

"This is the Chief Participant who runs this class," said Brightaloft, introducing one of the students.

"The subject for today," said the CP, "is *Oliver Tricks*. It's by
William Thickens; or is it Charles Darkery? Anyhow, you'll
know all about it in a few minutes."

He went to the podium and skillfully manipulated some levers.
The room went dark and silent. Then into this void burst a
blinding, deafening eruption of sights and sounds. Images projected from films writhed wildly over the walls, swirling, thump-
ing music poured into our ears, and flashes of multi-colored light
played intermittently over the audience, revealing excited faces,
hands waving in the air, and people jumping up to stand on the
seats. . ..

In the deafening music that accompanied all this, I thought I
could hear a dog barking, some excerpts from songs by the Sex
Pistols and "Please, sir, I want some more" sung to the tune of
"God Save the King."

"English culture, you know," said the CP. "We try to immerse
them in it." When the lights went on, he turned to me and said,
"Now for the discussion period."

Without any perceptible signal, one of the girls in the class
jumped onto the desk at the front of the room and did a remarkably animated dance representing "The Artful Dodger Working
the Crowd." . . . Next came a brief enactment of the murder of
Nancy; it involved a laser gun and spurts of blood that drenched
the first rows of the audience. The class cheered and applauded.

Anxious to meet the pedagogic genius who had planned this

audio-visual masterpiece, I asked Brightaloft, "Who is the professor of this class?"

"Professor?" repeated Brightaloft in a puzzled tone. It was apparently another archaism. He conferred with the CP for a moment, then brightened up. "What we want," he said "is the University Museum."

After a short swish on the Topographical Transformers, we stood in a display hall in front of three large glass cases, the first labelled "Professor, Male," the second, "Professor, Female," the third, "Unidentified." These were stuffed specimens, supported at the back by iron struts.

The Male Professor had been caught in mid-stride, while on his way to class, apparently. He wore a tattered deerstalker, and looked near-sightedly ahead of him from beneath a brow creased with wrinkles of perpetual inquiry. A drooping auburn mustache and a slack chin projected an expression of bemused casualness. He wore a frayed white shirt without a tie, a woolen zipper jacket, and a pair of baggy blue jeans with the "Levi-Strauss" written in script across one of the back pockets.

The Female Professor was somewhat stouter, and seemed to face her obsolescence with a mixture of optimism and benevolence. She had short brown hair, a pug nose, a wry smile emphasized with mauve lipstick, and a confident tilt to her head. She wore a pink leisure suit and a large pin that said "Don't Rubbish Australia," and carried in her hand a small brown paper sack that looked as if it contained a cheese sandwich and an apple.

The "Unidentified" specimen was a young male who was sitting down. He wore a sleeveless vest padded with down over a blue denim shirt, stuffed with ball-point pens and memorandum books . . .

"I see you're interested in that one," said Brightaloft, "We've never been able to learn what it is. We've never seen anything like it."

"I've seen them," I said, "It's a student."

"Marvellous!" exclaimed Brightaloft. "You seem to know a lot about these things."

"I've looked into them now and then," I said.

"Really?" said Brightaloft, "I had no idea. Who is your favorite author?"

"Thickens," I said, "or maybe Darkery. It doesn't really matter now."

iii

When I read my colleague's satire I was terribly moved: there was someone else in the department, someone whom I met and spoke to every day but did not know personally, whose thoughts and forebodings about the department, and presumably all English departments, were much like my own. I felt sad, and somehow guilty, that I could no longer help or be helped by this person, or by others in the department who might be trying to come to terms with Thickens and Darkery. When a student spoke to me about another member of the department who committed suicide in the late seventies—a man, the student explained, who seemed to take his teaching as seriously as I did—I had to acknowledge, reluctantly, that I had never done more than discuss the Seattle rain with the man while we waited for the elevator.

For the most part, however, I did not regret my isolation from the rest of the department—an isolation which was, by the early seventies, very nearly complete. I had never served on committees or been active in departmental affairs; my closest friends in the department had left, or retired, or died; and my ideas, my reputation, and my embattled position must have made me seem like an ominous figure to my newer colleagues. Why would anyone trying to make his way in the department wish to approach a man who not only seemed to have all kinds of monstrous ideas but also seemed to be against everything the department and the University were trying to do? Particularly when the man himself seemed quite content to go his own strange way without asking for anyone's help or friendship. My isolation, then, was partly circumstantial, partly of my own making; and I was, if not content with it, at least reconciled to it. For I had my own little Panzaic corner, and so long as I did not try to step out of it everyone seemed inclined to let me occupy it in peace. I was under no pressure to teach popular fiction, or to have student evaluations, or to do things differently or better. In fact my only serious conflicts with the department during these years were over the theses I supervised.

iv

Although I continued to experience ideological resistance in both my graduate and undergraduate classes during these years I never again had to withstand the kind of hostility I had encountered in the late sixties and early seventies. The hysteria, after peaking in the student riots, seemed to pass almost as quickly as it had appeared. To some extent, I suppose, the students were appalled by their own violence. For a period of weeks at Washington women in my classes were afraid to venture across campus and quite a few of the men were carrying guns. And they were, I believe, even more appalled by the police brutality which they either encountered or witnessed. It was not like TV; it was ugly and terrifying—in much the same way that Kent State proved to be ugly and terrifying. The campus revolution was not, as Watergate, for example, showed, changing the world; it was not even transforming the University in the ways the students had hoped it would. They continued to ride bicycles and carry backpacks, and a considerable number of them continued to champion their causes and recite their slogans. But not with the same fervor. They had become at least partially disillusioned and to that extent willing to concede a certain amount of academic freedom.

Yet their concessions never became more than partial. In 1972 James Q. Wilson argued that "the list of subjects that cannot be publicly discussed [at Harvard] in a free and open forum has grown steadily." (*Commentary*, June, 1972) And seven years later he was unable to say whether the intellectual climate had improved significantly. "Could Henry Kissinger or Arthur Jensen speak at Harvard today? . . . I hear phrases like 'Let's get a more responsible spokesman'—meaning someone more elusive and less doctrinaire. It worries me, deeply." (*Harvard Magazine*, March–April, 1979) And if Wilson had taken a look at Washington, or presumably any of the other state multiversities, he would have been even more worried. There the campus revolution did not die; it merely shed its hysteria, along with a number of its illusions, in favor of more restrained organizational attitudes.

For even this much change I was duly grateful, since it meant that I could go on meeting my classes—not with anything like the sense of intellectual freedom I had enjoyed before but without having to confront outright ideological hostility at every turn. Within a year after my disastrous seminar on "Love and Death" I could see that the graduate students were no longer in the same mood, that if I again encountered feminists as rabid as those who had filibustered my seminar they might pose a real nuisance, but they would never be able to gain the support necessary to make their tactics fully effective. Only a few of the graduate students were avidly clinging to their by now old causes, and the new cynics, with teaching jobs becoming more and more scarce, were busily transforming themselves into the new professionals, ready to play new and fashionable games in the form of Structuralist and Post-structuralist criticism.

The undergraduates too were following essentially the same patterns, aided and abetted by the new academic machinery that they themselves had helped to put into motion. The great majority of the students were coming to have less and less interest in matters intellectual which were not directly connected with geting ahead in the practical world—or, in their own jargon, with realizing their career objectives. It was almost as if, having witnessed the ineffectuality of those who had tried to resist the "system," they themselves had come to realize its omnipotence, and were now willing, even anxious, to capitulate to its demands. While not all of them were fully aware of the choices they were making, and why they were making them, a surprising number knew, or thought they knew, exactly what they were doing. And when, as I often did, I tried to point out the implications of their choices, I invariably had some student ready to set me straight: "Yes, they knew all that: they knew what organizational America might do to them. But what other choice did they have, short of being a freak or some kind of a bum?" Or as one quite bright Vietnam veteran put it: "Sure I'm joining up. I know it's like the Army. But if we're in society we're all in the social army, and since we're all in it, I want to make damned sure I'm an officer, not a private. I was a private in the U.S. Army; I'm going to be an officer in the organizational one."

Much as I sympathized with the individual students expressing these attitudes, I could see where they would certainly lead—where, in fact, they were already leading, most obviously in the University itself, which not only seemed incapable of maintaining what intellectual integrity it still possessed, but actually, in response to student and outside pressures, seemed bent on transforming many of its course offerings into those of a high-level technical or professional school. In literature, for example, the transformation was already taking place, as students who had formerly taken literature courses began choosing courses in psychology or sociology or anthropology or oceanography or geology—not because they believed these courses would be more interesting than literature, though possibly they found them to be so, but because they considered them to be more directly relevant to their new professional goals than literature. The one English course, apart from those in popular fiction, in which enrollments increased significantly during these years was Advanced Composition—a technical follow-up to Freshman Composition designed to increase the rhetorical skills of students in their various professional fields. That course, which burgeoned into a monster of innumerable sections, certainly helped to save jobs, but it also obliged professors to sacrifice their intellectual integrity still further. On two occasions I too had to teach the course to fill out my schedule: in my first effort I heard, for the first time in my life, the complaint that "the class wasn't getting its money's worth. They weren't there to fool around with ideas. They were there to learn how to write memorandums and stuff that would help them in their jobs." The next time I taught the course, anticipating the same complaint, I tried to make it clear to the students that I did not consider it my function to teach the writing of memorandums, that I considered the teaching of rhetoric apart from thought immoral, and that I hoped they were not determined to be immoral. At this point two students got up and walked out and the next day the enrollment in the class dropped from twenty-five to eleven, and the twelve of us then had what I considered a fairly interesting course. Not surprisingly that was the last time I was asked to teach Advanced Composition.

In taking my stand against the students I was not, I hasten to add, trying to stand on my dignity as a professor. Dignity had nothing to do with it. My point was that no one should have to do what the students were insisting that I do. Never, in all my years of teaching Freshman Composition, at five different universities, had I ever been expected to teach mechanics and rhetoric in and for themselves. Not even the Army, in Army English at Cornell, had expected that. Always there had been opportunities to show the connections between rhetoric and thought, rhetoric and feeling. And if the students now wished to evade or deny those connections it was, I believed, my obligation to deny their wishes. After all, the University had not, as yet, become a technical school, nor were English professors, as yet, required to function as pure technicians.

The only new concession I made to the students during these years was in the matter of grades—a concession which gave me no qualms whatsoever, since I had never believed in grades, never taken them seriously. If they all wanted C's to become B's and B's to become A's that was fine with me. In all else, however, I held the line, not on principle but because I felt certain that the students' new insistence upon organization (in the form of syllabuses, etc.) like their new insistence on gimmickry (in the form of arranging the chairs in a circle, etc.) represented an unconscious attempt on their part to turn the classes into TV—with the professor as a TV disc jockey, and with Dickens, say, becoming a novelistic prevision of "All In The Family."

All this I discussed with the students in the opening sessions of my classes before I tried to introduce them to my own approach. And while some of the students were indignant or dismayed and dropped my classes, quite a number of them stayed to hear me out, and a few showed genuine interest. Although the students I am speaking of had grown up with the campus revolution and its aftermath, and consequently had little if any sense of what classes had been like in earlier years, they could recognize that I was offering them something different, and a surprising number of them eventually went as far with me in the classroom and in their papers as even I could wish.

By the middle seventies, then, I could see the possibility of recapturing my undergraduate classrooms. And in some respects I did. But the experiences I had been through had taken their toll. I was no longer the person, or the teacher, I had been ten years earlier. Although my perceptions and my teaching skills were, I believe, sharper than ever before, I no longer had the enthusiasm, the trust, the belief that in the classroom I could go anywhere with the students. I found myself, at the beginning of each quarter, asserting my position so strongly that I undoubtedly scared away many students who might otherwise have been willing to try the Panzaic. In class I found that I had become at once more assertive and more wary—as if I had to ward off the kinds of difficulties I had been through when perhaps they were no longer actually there. And while I tried to check these tendencies I am not sure that I ever quite succeeded.

Even so I had a number of undergraduate classes during these years which were, in most respects, every bit as successful as any I had taught earlier. And if I had been equally successful in my graduate classes I might have felt encouraged enough to continue. But nearly all the graduate students had by the late seventies become so cautious, so geared to grades and getting ahead, that they were as impervious in their passivity as their predecessors had been in their hostility. If on occasion I stirred them into flurries of interest in my approach to Hardy or Lawrence or Theories of Fiction the interest quickly waned as the students began to realize where they were going, and what their going there meant. Perhaps I was expecting too much; perhaps I should have recognized that graduate classes could no longer be as free and exciting as those I had taught earlier, and then gone ahead to make the most of the possibilities which remained. That would have been the sensible thing to do. But I was no more sensible as I approached sixty-two, the age for early partial retirement, than I had been at twenty-two.

v

For all my difficulties I continued to have students who wished to have me supervise their theses. But in 1974 I decided that the time had come for me to give an unqualified "No" to their requests—as much for their sakes as mine. For the students who were already working with me were having to fight as never before for every inch of critical ground they tried to cover. In part the resistance they were encountering was no doubt directed at me through them, yet there was more to it than that. As the department was forced to meet popular demands in certain areas (by giving courses, for example, in everything from popular fiction to women's studies) it tried to maintain what it conceived to be traditional standards in the only places it still could. So that, paradoxically, the more free it became in its outward trappings the more conservative it became in its professional stance—until, by the middle seventies, the prevailing atmosphere in the department was, to all intents and purposes, indistinguishable from the Berkeley I had experienced in the late forties. The last thesis that I supervised, a Panzaic attempt to reinterpret three of George Eliot's novels, had to be rewritten in the light of such observations as these from the three faculty members who evaluated the work:

> We have [in the thesis] the harpings on "childhood freedom" and "childhood spontaneity," which seem to ignore what I had taken to be a well established truth that children are highly conventional.

> If what [the writer of the dissertation] argues is so, then Hetty [in *Adam Bede*] is a creation on the order of Satan. And finally, isn't it possible that were Hetty granted fulfillment of her pleasures, there would be a denial of any social order.

> It seems a gross distortion to try to argue the matter of "unrelenting social justice" as a dehumanizing force.

These and numerous other comments in the same vein, together with the arguments that accompanied them, convinced me that I could no longer encourage students to apply my critical approach in their theses. And I was thankful that I would no longer have to stand helplessly by while the students I supervised tried to fight battles which were more mine than theirs. As for the thesis itself, since, as the comments indicate, all three professors failed it, I had no choice in the end but to help the student revise his work to meet the various objections. And so ended this phase of my graduate teaching.

vi

For a time during the early seventies it looked as if my new version of the Panzaic, as I embodied it in several new critical essays, might alienate a number of my former students who were teaching at other universities. In 1972 I put the two parts of the Panzaic principle together in a single volume which I published at my own expense, a volume which also included explanatory afterwords by Gerald Butler and R. A. Brown. And in the same year I published the first draft of a long essay on *Wuthering Heights* in a new Panzaic journal, *Recovering Literature*, which Gerald Butler had started at San Diego State University. In this study of *Wuthering Heights* I tried to show that it is a unique novel, that the failure of Cathy's and Heathcliff's love simply cannot be accounted for in the terms in which the various characters try to account for it—or in the terms in which critics have tried to account for it:

> The kind of oneness Cathy and Heathcliff are striving for can only be realized through death and decomposition and reincarnation . . . No work, with the possible exception of Wagner's *Tristan und Isolde*, expresses the transcendence of love and death with greater power than *Wuthering Heights* . . . Finally, therefore, the novel achieves the end that I have defined as the end of all great fiction. But it does not achieve it by means of the Panzaic Principle, by using the real to undercut the ideal; rather what it does is to carry a particular ideal—the ideal of immaculate love—to such uncompromising extremes that it not only be-

comes magnificent in itself but also serves to undercut the pretensions of nearly all our other ideals. And it undercuts these other ideals so devastatingly that even "humanity" comes to be a term of opprobrium.

I thought highly of the essay. When it appeared in revised form in a Festschrift for Leonard Manheim (*Hartford Studies in Literature*, 1973) I even permitted myself to hope that it might gain a bit of general critical attention. I also thought highly of an essay on *Tess of the D'Urbervilles* which I published in *Recovering Literature* in 1972—an essay in which I tried to demonstrate that Tess's dilemma was not what previous critics had assumed, that she knew or sensed that she had responded to the villain, whom I described as not much more than a "walking talking phallus," in ways that neither she nor Hardy nor her society could begin to accept. The possibility that one or both of these essays would prove upsetting to those who shared my critical views doubtless crossed my mind, since what I was saying tended to contradict much of what had been written about the two novels in *Paunch*, but I was hardly prepared for Arthur Efron's two critical rejoinders. In the first, "Just What and Where is the Panzaic Principle in *Tess of the D'Urbervilles*? A Rebuttal to Wayne Burns," Efron mounted an attack in which he actually seemed bent on discrediting me as well as my criticism—an attack which prompted Gerald Butler, the editor of *Recovering Literature*, to come to my defense with a counterattack on Efron. At this juncture it seemed as if there were going to be two warring Panzaic journals; and when, in 1974, two other former students, Eugene Dawson and Raymond Mize, helped establish still another critical journal, *Sphinx*, at the University of Saskatchewan, I had visions of a three-sided war. But *Sphinx*, although it had Panzaic leanings, did not acknowledge any direct Panzaic connections, and therefore did not enter into the controversy.

Although I hated to see our tiny Panzaic band split in two, I tried to convince myself that the split might in the long run prove beneficial, if only it could be worked out amicably. After all, Warren Tallman, Calvin Bedient and other former students had rejected the Panzaic without any hard feelings or recriminations on their part or mine. And while Efron was going much further, in that he was developing another version of the Panzaic in opposition to mine, I could accept that too, so long as he did not try to impose his version on my criticism. Since I had always refused to trim my perceptions to fit my own notions of the Panzaic I could hardly trim them to fit someone else's. A cardinal point of my critical approach had always been that the body, or the guts, could never be considered holy. If, in a particular novel, I found that the guts were not right after all, as I did in *Wuthering Heights*, I had to say so, regardless of what happened to the body or the Principle—or, for that matter, regardless of what effect my saying so had on what I or other Panzaic critics had previously written. Otherwise the Panzaic principle would become another critical blueprint, useful for getting literature into line with our philosophical preconceptions but not very useful for revealing what goes on in serious novels.

Perhaps I should have said all this at the time, in an effort to clear up further misunderstandings. As things turned out, however, I may have chosen the better part of wisdom in remaining silent, and continuing on as before with my criticism. Over the next several years I published studies of *The Fox, Vanity Fair, Jude the Obscure*, and *The Woodlanders* in *Recovering Literature*—all without creating any further misunderstandings. And then, to my great pleasure and surprise, Efron wrote to ask me if I would be willing to have John Doheny and Jerald Zaslove act as guest editors of *Paunch* in bringing out a Wayne Burns issue devoted to my criticism and teaching.

It was a great honor, and when the volume itself appeared in 1977 (*Paunch*, No. 46–47), with Sancho and the good Don on the front cover, I thought the issue might well have been entitled, after Lawrence, *Look, We Have Come Through*. For the volume was not a Festschrift, not elegiac in tone: it looked forward, as well as back, in a spirit as positive as the world we live in would allow. The contributions of my former students who had become my close friends were those I appreciated the most but I also thought highly of Gordon P. Turner's "The God-father I Don't Know," since it made me feel that my defeat as a teacher in the late sixties and early seventies had not erased my earlier work, that others were continuing on where I was leaving off:

> I don't know Wayne Burns. I've never met him. I've never heard him speak. Nor have I been to the University of Washing-ton where he teaches or to the houseboat he calls home. And yet I have a sense of Wayne Burns, of the physicality and com-passion of the man, of the capacity of TEACHER his name evokes, of the strength of his neo-romantic critical beliefs, of the close feeling that exists between him and those who have been his students. . . . It is a fact that to many second generation stu-dents of literature like myself Wayne Burns is the godfather. I know the creed that his adherents teach. I know that when I meet the asinine and the inflexible in life, I can function because of the particular attitude toward life I've gained through reading literature with my "guts" under the guidance of his followers. I know that the family who attached themselves to what Wayne Burns believes in are out there teaching at this moment, and long ago I became a member of that circle, familiar with its nuances, and myself extending Burns' ideas.

I was also pleased with Efron's comments on my work, be-ginning with his acknowledgment of his anger. "What was going on," he explained, "was my increasing anger over the 'failure' of my father-figure to carry out the goals I had attri-buted to him . . . I have given up the attempt to tell Burns how to do his work." Actually, as Efron's further comments reveal, he could never quite give up the attempt, yet he bestowed un-stinting praise on much of my criticism, including the study of Hardy's *The Well Beloved* that I contributed to the volume, and he concluded most graciously:

> I remain indebted for the great deal he has done, and I'm sure I'll continue to learn from what he will write yet. He is the first literary critic in America to understand the importance of the body in the novel . . . I only hope that in my efforts to do the

theory in my own way I don't lose the gut-level, the immediacy that isn't ever going to be acceptable.

The last time I taught *The Panzaic Principle*, a graduate student who already had an M.A. (in creative writing), and who was just getting interested in criticism, took very strongly to Burns' approach. . . . He asked me, when the course was about over, "Who else does criticism of the kind Burns does?" I thought the question over for a moment. The answer, really, just had to be, "No one."

The Wayne Burns issue did so much to revive my spirits that when, in the spring of 1978, I was invited to give a lecture at Western Washington University on "a literary subject" I decided to stretch the subject a bit and talk about the teaching of literature:

> Tonight I would like to begin by sharing with you some of my thoughts and feelings and doubts about what, as a professor of English, has been my primary purpose in life—the teaching of literature, and more specifically, the teaching of fiction. And then, after considering some of the difficulties I have encountered and observed, I shall try to suggest a few possible answers that may, I hope, prove interesting and perhaps even beneficial.

What I then said, although it may have been all right as a lecture, left me with the feeling that I had only begun to say what needed to be said. When I gave the talk again, at Simon Fraser University, I had the same feeling, only stronger. And when the talk was later published in the *West Coast Review* (April, 1979), with an afterword by Jerald Zaslove in which he stressed the need for me to say more, in another talk or essay, I felt I had to try. And I did. But I soon realized that my thoughts and feelings about the teaching of literature would not fit into an essay; that if I were going to express them at all adequately I would have to show how they developed from and related to everything else in my life—from my sense of myself and the students to my sense of literature and criticism and the university and the world. And that is what I have attempted to do.

A Final Note
(1979–1982)

When, in 1979, the department voted me Professor Emeritus, and the University, in typical organizational fashion, reclassified me as a part-time employee, thereby stripping me of the few privileges and benefits professors enjoy, I felt that I had, to all intents and purposes, left the classroom forever. While I knew that I would, for purely economic reasons, have to go through my old teaching motions in at least two undergraduate classes per year, I never expected the teaching to be much more than a sad or perhaps even a traumatic reminder of what I had given my life to for almost forty years.

But it hasn't turned out that way. The six classes I have taught here and at San Diego State have all been far more sympathetic to my Panzaic approach than I anticipated; indeed three of the six, to my great delight and gratification, have actually been as responsive as my best classes of fifteen or twenty years ago. And while I obviously cannot, on the basis of my experiences in these few classes, offer any conclusive evidence that students in the humanities have changed much over the past several years, I sincerely believe that they have—that their militant ideals and beliefs, the ideals and beliefs which they carried over from the seventies, have finally worn so woefully thin that many of them are once again willing to go all the way with any teacher who will brave the dark woods with them.

Index